The SAP Blue Book

A Concise Business Guide to the World of SAP

The

A Concise Business Guide to the World of SAP

Michael Doane

The SAP Blue Book

This book was written by Michael Doane.

"SAP" is a registered trademark of SAP Aktiengesellschaft, Systems, Applications and Products in Data Processing, Neurottstrasse 16 69190 Walldorf, Germany. The publisher gratefully acknowledges SAP's kind permission to use its trademark in this publication. SAP AG is not the publisher of the book and is not responsible for it under an aspect of press law.

Published by Michael Doane

Printed in the United States.

ISBN 1-57579-125-0

First Edition, revised

First Printing, April 1998

Second Printing, July 1998

CONTENTS

Preface...1

Chapter 1: How SAP Discovered the New World 5

A Brief History of Business Computing
A Quarter Century of Partial Victories
The Accelerating Failure of Traditional Information Systems
Computerize This
How SAP Discovered the New World
How SAP Rose to the Top
SAP By the Numbers
"That's in the Next Release" - The SAP R&D Steamroller

Chapter 2: What is SAP? 23

The Shelf Life of This Chapter is Questionable
Coping with the SAP Alphabet
Features of SAP
Core Business Applications of SAP
Workflow Applications
And All the Rest
Critical Distinctions Between SAP and What You Know
SAP is the On-Ramp; Workflow is the Highway

Chapter 3: SAP in a Microwave 55

A New System Life Cycle
SAP in a Microwave
Post Implementation: The Windfall
One Size Fits All (With Reservations)
Certified Business Solutions
How Rapid SAP R/3 Implementation Methods Can Be Misleading

Chapter 4: The Wild West of SAP Consulting.................93

A Brief History of SAP Consulting in North America
What SAP Consultants Do
When SAP is $AP
Choosing Your SAP Consultants Wisely
Trends in SAP Consulting
Post-Adolescence for SAP Consulting

Chapter 5: Learning to Swim in the SAP Sea 111

Swimming Lessons or Lifeboats
Executives Are Seldom Taught But They Can Learn
Education for Middle Management
Course Customization, Environments and Supports
Modes of Education
Project Team Training
Skills Migration for IS Staff
End User Training
The Cost of SAP Education
The Cost of Lousy Training

Chapter 6: The Cost of the Journey 131

Now We Know Better
Predictable Costs 1: Software
Predictable Costs 2: Hardware
Estimating Software and Hardware Costs
Consulting Costs and How to Control Them
Budget Modeling for SAP Implementations
Executive Oversight and the High Cost of SAP
Post Script: SAP, Showgirls, and the Chicago Cubs

Chapter 7: Hearts, Minds, Pink Slips & Career Paths...153

Throwing Yourself on the SAP Sword
Communicating Change
We Had a Meeting and You Weren't There

Chapter 8: The Life Expectancy of SAP 165

What's Wrong With SAP?
The Backlash Gives Birth to Team SAP
More Wives than Brigham Young

Afterward 173

SAP P.S. 177

Red Light, Green Light: Are You Ready?
Alternative Life Styles
SAP Competitors
Useful Web Sites
SAP Newsgroups
SAP Bibliography
Glossary of Terms

Acknowledgments

There are no Renaissance people in the world of SAP. The subject is too wide and too deep. Specialization, combined with individual experience, leads to wisdom and I am grateful for the generous, enthusiastic, and wise assistance that has been provided.

I thank Joe Mierau of Pine Hill Press for his calm faith and aesthetic help, Dick McCarthy for his humor and guidance, Michelle Bush for her confidence and clarity, and all of the contributors for their generous sharing of insight and experience: Betty Costa, Mark Dendinger, Nancy Bancroft, Jon Reed, Carol Martin, Peter Steiner, Pat Wade, and David Chapman.

And finally, my deepfelt thanks to Rob Doane, *frère et complice,* to whom this book is dedicated.

If you come to a fork in the road, take it.
Yogi Berra

I didn't say all the things I said.
Yogi Berra

PREFACE

In late August of 1997, I found myself wandering through Disney World, in Orlando, Florida, on a calm and warm Sunday evening. All the usual icons were on colorful display: Mickey, Goofy, Donald, dwarves, chipmunks, pirates, and princesses. The lights were lit, the flowers bounteous, and the troops of Disney hosts and hostesses as buoyant and numerous as ever. All the same, this was not the usual Disney scene. Despite the bouncy strains of 'Hakuna Matata', the atmosphere was muted, placid, and definitely lacking in boisterous mirth. At first glance, I could not tell what was amiss. Only after about half an hour was it clear to me: *there were no children there.* Only adults, roughly fourteen thousand of them, most between the ages of 25 and 55.

Had this been an episode from The X-files, it might have been titled 'SAPphire '97, the Welcoming'.

SAPphire is the annual convention for SAP clients, consultants, suppliers, and partners and SAP America had rented DisneyWorld that Sunday evening as a way of rolling out the red carpet to all of us. That night, the size and scope of the SAP world was encapsuled in that promising but weird scene of fourteen thousand business adults occupying a child-oriented theme park.

Promising, but weird. That pretty well sums up the feeling we all have when first confronted with SAP.

In order to put the accent more on the promise and less on the weirdness, it helps to find information that will enlighten you. For a subject as wide and deep as SAP, it is not surprising to find that there is a wealth of information about the product, loads of marketing material about the company, technical white papers, seminars, conferences, websites and newsgroups, but I am constantly being asked to 'put it into a nutshell' or to explain to an executive who asks 'what does this mean to me?'

Is SAP a fad or a phenomenon? Are firms snapping it up because of its merits or because of a lemming effect? Will the explosion of SAP licensing continue or will the firm be overcome by its competitors in the client/server market? Is SAP only for large firms or can small firms gain benefit from it?

A consultant's favorite, and often necessary, answer to thorny questions is 'it depends'. But just as important questions do not always yield to pat answers, an understanding of SAP is not gleaned in a single meeting or seminar.

Years ago, I was the IS manager for Europe for a major English electronics and defense firm. Monthly meetings were held in Brussels, including managing directors and finance directors. At each meeting, I was afforded one half hour to report progress for our European-wide systems implementation and I noted that once the subject turned from commercial and financial subjects to 'computers', half of my audience immediately went into *the zone* and I was only surprised not to hear outright snoring.

The same reaction occurs with most managers when the subject of SAP comes up. The misconception is that it is a computer subject, when in reality it is very much a business subject. The consequence of this misconception is that many firms have failed to implement and use SAP's R/3 because of management presumptions that R/3 is just the current hot software and that it should be implemented just as other software has been implemented.

For the past few years I have offered a management seminar in SAP, targeted to middle management and up, which covers most of the subjects explored in this book. The original seminar lasted two days but few business people feel they can sacrifice that much time for a subject they think they could master in less. The seminar has since been recast for a single day and even that one day is often difficult for an executive to invest. I have been asked on more than one occasion to give a half-day seminar and once I was asked to scale down the seminar to *one hour*. In a nutshell.

This book is intended to provide that nutshell for those of you who desperately need to understand the business world of SAP but who do not have the time or inclination to attend a seminar. It is an objective view, drawn from direct experience, observation, and collaboration, and offers SAP from a business perspective, not a technical perspective. That is not to say that 'technology' will not make an appearance. One of the more heartfelt themes in what follows is that there is no longer a gulf between business and technology; further, the bridging of that gulf is why we have so many new subjects to master.

As we move closer to the new millennium, notions of revolutions, breakthroughs, new eras, and transformations are proliferating. It is difficult to separate truth from hype, so let's return to one of the questions listed earlier: is SAP a fad or a phenomenon? The answer is, it is a phenomenon, and a welcome one at that. Whether or not you or your firm can take advantage of this phenomenon and what it might take for you to do so should be among the more important questions of the era. But first you need to know what the animal is, how to feed it, what makes it bite, and the language behind the roaring. You want it concise and to the point.

Herein is your nutshell.

Michael Doane, March, 1998

CHAPTER 1

How SAP Discovered the New World

⌐ A Brief History of Business Computing

⌐ A Quarter Century of Partial Victories

⌐ The Accelerating Failure of Traditional Information Systems

⌐ Computerize This

⌐ How SAP Discovered the New World

⌐ How SAP Rose to the Top

⌐ SAP by the Numbers

⌐ "That's in the Next Release" - The SAP R&D Steamroller

How SAP Discovered the New World

A Brief History of Business Computing

YEAR	WHAT WE CALLED IT	LASTING ICON	ENDURING NERD SYMBOL
1960	DP Data Processing	Punch cards	Buddy Holly thick lenses
1970	EDP Electronic DP	Ugly green screens	Pocket Protector
1980	IT Information Technology	Bar codes	Flowchart Template
1990	IS	Laptop Solitaire	BMW

A Quarter Century of Partial Victories

"Any sufficiently advanced technology is indistinguishable from magic," wrote Arthur C. Clarke in the early 1960's.

A stellar concept. But what if the word 'sufficiently' is removed? The magic vanishes.

Since the 1960's, twin notions have rested side by side: computer and nerd. The nerd with the pocket protector and a brace of colored pencils. The nerd with coke-bottle lens glasses held together at the bridge of the nose with scotch tape. The nerd who controls the programs that control the nervous system of the business. For over a quarter century, the nerd has been, if not your enemy, your bete noire, that pointy pebble in your business shoe, that reluctant, indecipherable human conduit between your information needs and your business satisfaction.

Through the years, the nerds have metamorphosed. Their languages have changed from Cobol and Fortran to RPG III and Basic and on to C++. Those coke bottle lenses are now contacts and the pocket protectors have long since been shed in favor of a light pen and the manly mouse. The nerds are no longer merely programmers or systems analysts, they are data base administrators, horizontal integration specialists, enterprise reengineers, network administrators, or majority stockholders in Microsoft.

All the same, the notion persists that computers and the systems that run on them are the domain of nerds and that business people are still at their mercy. But it not so.

A number of evolutionary breakthroughs, engineered by the nerds themselves, have contributed to a sea change in the way information systems are

> "the volume of computer-managed analytical data is doubling every 18-24 months"
> Meta Group 1/97

implemented, exploited, and maintained. Client/server technology, object-oriented programming, Internet and other telecom-related advances, as well as technologies that take advantage of all of these strides, have left us with a new business topography that is only recently coming clear to those of us in the business of information technology.

Key items on the new map include:

❑ A change in the role of business people vis-à-vis the information systems intended to support them.

❑ A corresponding power shift for the information systems people (the nerds in question).

❑ A radical shift in the life cycle of information systems.

What has not changed, and what must change, is the attitude that most executives have in regard to information itself. Beyond the vision, the creation, and the implementation of information systems is the real nut of the deal: the use or abuse of information systems. Too many firms gather, store, and analyze information about themselves in a university-of-us fashion, with one study leading to another. For a business to be truly successful, and for that success to be maintained over time, information should be a catalyst for *informed* action.

The Accelerating Failure of Traditional Information Systems

Misconceptions on the part of business people about the complexity of information systems and a parallel arrogance on the part of many systems people have led to a growing antagonism between these two groups. Whichever side you are coming from, you know the scenario.

❑ The business group, often represented by a steering committee, demands new services. The IS group steps up to the plate and negotiations begin.

❑ The business group's ability to define the needed services is limited to a business point of view, but the IS people are asking detailed questions (field lengths, sort orders, interfacing rules, procedural rules). The business people seldom have the time or knowledge to adequately answer all of these questions. The IS people have to make decisions in their stead.

❑ Functional specifications are approved by the business group and turned over to the 'techies' for a round of technical specifications, programming, and testing.

❑ Direct users are trained. Data is loaded to the new system or converted from existing systems.

❑ In the interim, months have passed, business eons. The newly-installed system is geared to win last year's war and the business people are already asking for changes. Systems people argue that they have delivered what business asked for. The cycle of antagonism and disappointment continues.

This same cycle has visibly accelerated over the past ten years, during which time business has grown more and more complex. The frustrations of both business people (demand) and systems people (supply) have grown accordingly. At lunch time, a sales director reads an article in a biz journal about gee-whiz new technology and how it is going to change the face of sales and then returns to his

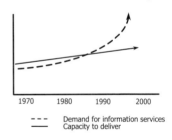

Demand for information services
Capacity to deliver

desk to mull over a month-old printout of 'hot' prospects. A committee of directors puts the seal of approval on a restructuring plan that will save their firm millions over the first six months only to find that the systems needed to support the restructuring may take twelve months to build and implement.

"When I put my foot on the gas, nothing happens," complains an oil refinery CEO. Many hundreds of thousands of executives have shared this thought over the past quarter century. Companies have often been doomed to move according to the speed of their information systems, a relative snail's pace when a simple jog would yield a fortune.

Partial victories have come every two to four years. Consider the following technological leaps and how the success promised by each has been compromised:

The stand-alone desktop computer became commonplace in the mid 1980's and promised vast economies in the financial and administrative arena and a dispersal of data centers from the data processing departments to individual users. The economies have been realized, as has a certain democratization of information, but there has been another edge to this very sharp sword: the cacophony of data that emanates from "personal" computers. We see renegade profit & loss analyses unscroll from printers on shop floors, sixteen-color bar charts generated by accounting staff that "prove" the need to eliminate product lines, and enough 9 point spreadsheets with decimals and percentages to wallpaper the Grand Canyon. My computer says . . . oh yeah, well *my* computer says...

The PC network, which quickly followed the rise of the stand-alone desktop, was accompanied by bold predictions of 'paperless companies', in which the volume of business data would expand but the paper needed to carry it would contract (much in the same way credit cards 'expanded' purchasing power while diminishing the need for wrinkled dollar bills.) While it is true that PC networks eliminate much of the data redundancy that once existed and have clearly served us well in the realm of data sharing and transmission, it is equally true that companies like International Paper and Georgia Pacific are doing more business than ever in 8 1/2 x 11 paper products.

(In the same fashion, we find that the Internet has not, and will not replace our love of newsprint and the feel of a paperback in our hands. We will not wean ourselves from *hard* copy all too soon.)

PC-Mainframe connections promised a consistency of data in which PC users or user groups could tap into the mainframe well for raw enterprise data and analyze it with powerful PC tools. But these connections have only led to an acceleration of data 'noise' rather than information, and the claim that the raw data comes from 'the computer' has been compromised by the manipulation of that data with the PC.

The dispersion of data entry from centralized "keypunch" to source entry, whether via keyboard, barcode reader, or scanner has fulfilled the promise of vastly improved data integrity and rapid data capture. The other side of this shiny coin has been the emerging need to train systems users to ever more sophisticated functions. The failure here has not been technological and cannot be pinned on the nerds; it is the failure of business (read=management) to sufficiently grasp the need for education. The notion of user training as the key to success with new systems has long since been surpassed by the reality of systems use: education at various levels is a necessity to which most firms only give lip service.

The shift from centralized (mainframe) to distributive processing (smaller computers in a network) has delivered faster local turnaround for data and allowed for applications that better fit user group needs. Specific software has been acquired and often customized for specific needs. However, distributive processing has also led to a massive multiplication of interfaces, not only site-to-site interfaces, but also between software packages of disparate origin.

One highly visible failure of distributive processing, as opposed to centralized, has been the decay of corporate-level management information. The timeliness of data collection is always questionable and the accuracy of the data suspect. This failure can be squarely pinned on the insoluble and costly burden of interfacing.

The ascendance of the CIO during the 1980's signaled a welcome departure from a hierarchical structure in which information systems were the domain of finance people. For the first time, companies stopped looking at 'data processing' as an overhead and began to see it as a reducer of overhead. However, once freed from the shackles of finance, information specialists discovered the dark side of their new autonomy: ceaseless, unanswerable demand by business people for better business systems.

By the early part of this decade, we had arrived at what constituted an information stalemate. In sum, our distributed systems were unmanageable, our data unreliable, and our systems staff increasingly unable to deliver new systems supports in a timely fashion. And then along came SAP R/3.

Computerize This

CEOs do not spend much of their time thinking about computer technology. Their muse time tends to embrace competitive analyses, potential acquisitions, corporate restructuring, and the fluctuating value of their stock options.

Senior executives are on pretty much the same paper cloud, although their focus will naturally descend to their patch of turf, a corporate division, a product line, a geographic sector, or whatever. Few are interested in the day-to-operations of a company and if you review the last half dozen projects your company has undertaken, you will probably find that they were instigated by employees below the senior management borderline.

All the same, the systems that you have today reflect past management decisions and the systems that you have tomorrow will reflect today's management decisions.

There may be a coterie amongst you who believe that SAP R/3 is the wide doorway through which your firm can enter a more productive and profitable future. Without the consent and understanding of senior management, that door will never be cracked open.

By the same token, "computerize this" has too often been a management order in firms that are failing. Computerization will not help half as much as a change in business processes. In fact, computerization alone can be disastrous. A company that is losing money with slow and inefficient data systems can accelerate their losses with fast and efficient data systems.

How SAP Discovered the New World

I never thought I would see myself as any kind of a pioneer, but in the realm of micro-computing, I have to admit that I go way back, all the way to 1980, the year I first touched a TRS 80 and blinked some Basic code across a hazy green screen. Shortly thereafter, I was introduced to the miracle of VisiCalc (the Adam of spreadsheets) and I used a Commodore Pet that possessed all of 64K of memory. Once VisiCalc was loaded, I was left with 12K and a little memory counter in the lower left of the screen that would deflate to 8K or 6K once I keyed in an "exotic" formula like @Sum(A1..A14).

What makes me feel like a pioneer is the relative power, and cost, of micro-computing nowadays. (I used the word 'nowadays'. Isn't that a pioneer-style word?) I no longer have a memory counter to deal with and 64K is chump change in a world now measured in gigabytes. The laptop which is mother to this book has 48MB of memory and I have made a three-dimensional spreadsheet that offers every possible imagined statistic for my fantasy baseball team, yet I still have miles of memory available.

My status as pioneer is only as a business user. More clever technical folks were fiddling with gizmo computers since well before 1980. In the spring of 1973, design work was completed on the Micral, the first non-kit computer based on a microprocessor (the Intel 8008). Built in France, the Micral was advertised in the U.S., but was not successful there. The term itself "micro-computer" is often attributed to the apparition of the Micral, but may well have resulted from the fact that during this same period there was a major distinction between mainframe systems and minis (this being the period of time in which distributive processing was all the rage), so these little tykes had to be referred to as micro-computers. In the interim, we have progressed from desktops to luggables to laptops to palmtops but this evolution has not yet led us to develop the pin-like fingers necessary for some of the keyboards included with these itsy-bitsy computers.

		Memory	Storage	Applications	1997 $
1980	TRS 80	64K	256K	Basic	$3000
1982	Commodore Pet	128K	256K	Visicalc	$4000
1985	IBM PC XT	512K	10 MB	Lotus, Wordperfect	$4000
1989	Victor Luggable	1 MB	400 MB	Lotus, WP, DB4	$4000
1995	Dell Portable	16 MB	1 GB	Lotus, WP, DB4, Internet	$4000
1997	Gateway Laptop	48 MB	2 GB	The whole she-bang	$4500

The author's micro-computer geneology

In past decades, storage space and memory had to be carefully managed and cutting corners with record sizes was a part of every analyst's daily life. One result of space management is the Year 2000 debacle that so many companies are facing right now. The savings of those two digits "19" before each year entry may not now seem to be of any import, but before client/server technology came along (as well as the evolution of storage media) two digits per record times 100,000 records was 200K of saved space! That 200K is now a whiff of air, but twenty years ago, the term gigabyte only applied to supercomputers and floppy diskettes were just coming onto the scene.

At any rate, the processing power of all computers has taken generational leaps just about every two years since 1980. In this same time frame, connectivity between micro-computers and mainframes has also had a rapid evolution. This connectivity issue is yet another facet of the decline of Apple. Macs generally talk only to each other, seldom to big daddy mainframes.

In the mid 1980's, data could be directly downloaded from mainframes to PCs. This major step was followed by transactional connectivity and, by the early 1990's, to client/server technology. These days, mainframes and desktops can be configured so that applications, data, and presentation servers can be tuned to company traffic and needs. Scalability is accordion-like as processing power can be moved from the mainframe to individual desktops or separate networks and back again.

In terms of applications software, there has not been an evolution to parallel that of processing power. Various software suppliers have tended to churn out packages that have been limited to single platforms (HP or DEC or IBM), thus requiring prospective clients to have the platform in question if they want to use the software. During these same years, distributive processing was the norm, in which individual company sites had their own hardware and soft-ware and data consolidations were made via interfaces.

> SAP has become the Columbus of the information systems world. The company sailed west with the powers of micro-computing and east with the complete and integrated applications suite and met at a median point we know as client/server technology.

As a result, companies today have a variety of platforms and operating systems, a variety of applications written in various languages, and a tangled web of interfaces holding it all together (or not).

Slowly, and at first quietly, SAP AG built something different. Four engineers broke away from IBM Germany and began peddling a mainframe financial package in 1972. In 1976, they tacked on a materials management module that was integrated with the financials. There followed a sales and distribution module, then production planning, and inevitably more and more application modules. Each succeeding module remained fully integrated with the others and the understandable popularity of this horizontal integration led to the rise of SAP AG throughout Europe, South Africa, and Australia.

The system in question, referred to as R/2, was a mainframe package that did not catch on in North America, but SAP AG had continued its march toward having an integrated suite of applications at a critical point in time.

The two evolutionary curves that were most prominent in the mid 1980's were the power of micro-computing and the crying need for applications that could be integrated without the complications and costs of interfacing.

SAP AG took note of these two evolutionary curves and, with the announcement of R/3 in late 1992, it has become the Columbus of the information systems world. Banking on the revolutionary premise that business processes are not vertical, but are flat (horizontal), the company sailed west with the powers of micro-computing and east with the complete and integrated applications suite and met at a median point we know as client/server technology.

How SAP Rose to the Top

Brilliance, innovation, and daring are seldom sufficient for the launching of a business phenomenon. Luck (otherwise known as the confluence of events) played a major role in the early stratospheric climb of R/3 licensing. In 1993, just as R/3 was gaining a foothold in North America, Michael Hammer and James Champy published *Reengineering the Corporation, A Manifesto for Business Revolution.* Over the next year and a half, over 1.7 million copies of this book were sold, with nearly half of this total attributed to North America. In brief, Hammer and Champy describe the need for businesses to radically re-invent themselves in order to bring about dramatic improvements in performance. The accent is on the word *radical*. They compare reorganizations and structural tinkering to 'rearranging the deck chairs on the Titanic' and seek to demonstrate that business processes rather than organizational structures are the subject at hand.

The simplicity and brilliance of this message are confounded by the fact that it is still very hard to reinvent an existing company. Company traditions and culture, executive turf protection, conflicting strategies, and natural corporate inertia all tend to resist radical reengineering. Further (and generally ignored in the Hammer and Champy opus) information systems have to be radically recast to support full-scale reengineering. This is where the announcement of R/3 could not have come at a better time. CEOs leaped at R/3 as a means to the promised land of what is now commonly referred to as BPR.

SAP marketing followed this trend to the letter as sales efforts have targeted senior management rather than information systems management; that is to say, SAP sells its software as a business solution, not a technology solution.

The announcement of SAP R/3 with client/server and workflow coincided with the vast wave of "downsizing" that began in the late 1980's. As unimaginative as downsizing can be, it leaves in its wake a need for the survivors to re-invent how their company will continue to function. It is, according to the Hammer and Champy vision, sufficiently radical. It should not be surprising to realize that, in 1993 and 1994, SAP R/3 was seen as a CEO's 'downsizing partner'. In reality, SAP's product is no such thing, but the perception did no harm whatever to sales.

More cogent to the success of SAP are 1) the high quality and flexibility of its product, 2) a rigid devotion to research and development, and 3) its strategy partnerships with platform vendors, consulting firms, and competitors.

SAP by the Numbers

In 1992, just before R/3 was announced, SAP America's revenues were $180M. Final 1997 revenues were in the neighborhood of $1.4B. Worldwide, SAP has followed the same trend. There are now over 13,000 SAP R/3 installations worldwide, with North America claiming a third of them. Worldwide

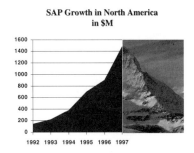

SAP Growth in North America in $M

SAP revenues exceeded $3.6 billion in 1997, up from $2.6 billion in 1996. Conservative estimates for 1998 point to continued growth and it is possible that SAP AG revenues will reach the five billion dollar mark.

Until 1992, when R/3 was introduced, the great majority of SAP licenses were in Europe, with a smattering of others in Australia, South Africa, and North America. Since that time, as SAP support for both R/3 and English has improved, North America has come to represent the most important part of SAP revenues.

At the end of 1997, the company employed 12,860 people, an increase of 40% from 1996. SAP America added 900 new employees for a total of 2,600 employees at the year end. SAP expects to increase its worldwide headcount by 5,000 in 1998.

In essence, SAP sells in the neighborhood of two hundred licenses each month. This activity represents about two-thirds of their revenue with the remainder coming from consulting and training. It is important to note that most software suppliers do not sell half this many licenses in a year.

SAP's product has long been
viewed as a Big Boy Toy, better
suited to Gigacorp than to Mom
and Pop, Inc. Reversing this notion
has been a major preoccupation of
SAP's through the mid 1990's and
the truth is, SAP's growth is across
the board in terms of company size.

Company Size	% of SAP
> $2.5B	18%
$1B - $2.5K	17%
$500M- $1B	11%
$200M - $500M	18%
< $200M	36%

Source: SAP

Whereas R/2 was a big hit in Europe, Australia, and South Africa
but not much of a mover elsewhere, R/3 has thrust SAP into an
international limelight. The two fastest-growing markets for SAP in
1997 were Asia and South America.

It should be noted that some of the fuel to this fire is the Y2K
crisis. Companies facing the need to correct existing software are
finding it preferable to throw out old systems and SAP has been a
popular new choice. As the millennium approaches, it is possible
that new licenses will begin to flatten out. All the same, SAP
continues to offer evolutions of its own self (new functionality,
new features) and the financial outlook remains cloudless.

"That's in the Next Release"-The SAP R&D Steamroller

Legend has it that through its quarter century of existence SAP
AG has religiously invested 25% of its annual revenues in research
and development. With 1997 revenues in the range of $3 billion,
that would translate to $750 million, which roughly equals the total
revenue of Peoplesoft, one of SAP's prime competitors. Following
the same math, SAP had 1995-1996 revenues totaling more than $4
billion and so would already have spent $1 billion on research and
development over the past two years. What a company does with
R&D money will largely determine its staying power in the
marketplace. In two years, SAP has:

⌐ delivered AS/400 versions of R/3

⌐ announced industry-specific versions for IS Oil, Automotive, and Retail, to name a few

⌐ introduced North American HR and payroll

⌐ delivered R/3, version 3.1 (the Internet version)

⌐ delivered the Accelerated SAP method

⌐ introduced Business Engineering Workbench

⌐ announced R/3, version 4

⌐ instituted the Certified Business Solutions program.

This is only a partial list, but you get the idea. New wrinkles and tucks of SAP product are announced weekly, and major announcements quarterly.

Says David Chapman, the SAP project manager at Lyondell-Citgo Refining Company: " Don't expect SAP to have it all. Some of the functionality you want just will not be there. You will need other tools. SAP has recognized this and there is now a peripheral industry of add-on, bolt-ons, and industry-specific tools that might well fill your gaps."

For years software sales people have answered the majority of client queries about functionality with the evasive, "That's in the next release." With SAP software, this claim just may be true.

CHAPTER 2

What is SAP?

⌐ The Shelf Life of This Chapter is Questionable

⌐ Coping with the SAP Alphabet

⌐ Features of SAP

⌐ Core Business Applications of SAP

⌐ Workflow Applications

⌐ And All the Rest

⌐ Critical Distinctions Between SAP and What You Know

⌐ SAP is the On-Ramp; Workflow is the Highway

What is SAP?

The Short Answer

Applications, Features, Marketing, and Mysticism.

The Shelf Life of This Chapter is Questionable

As any good SAP-watcher knows, no moss grows under those munchkin feet in Walldorf, Germany and Foster City, California where SAP R&D takes place. Even as I type this paragraph at 120 wpm, ABAP/4 code is coursing through SAP pipelines and wrapping itself into beta releases and SAP Dot Com announcements. Veterans of SAP implementations will remember that version 3.0 releases a through g came available within roughly a 14 month span in 1995-1996. No book could keep up with a thousand bit-byte ABAP/4 zombies, and this book will not try. Even as this book goes to print, new SAP releases will render any description of the product woefully incomplete.

This first section covers some of the basics of SAP, the company, and R/3, the product.

If you already are familiar with the basics, skip to the next section.

Coping with the SAP Alphabet

Within the world of SAP, there are many variations on the meaning of the letters S A P.

To the paranoid, it is a German code for "Thanks for the Deutschmarks." To a careless reader, it is Spa misspelled. To a disgruntled customer, Shut up And Pay. To a concerned project manager, Say A Prayer. To the competition, Sulk And Pout. To an SAP consultant, Suitcase And Passport.

Ess Ay Pee is how it is pronounced, not sap as in rap, cap, or slap. And all it means is Systems, Applications, and Products. Pretty boring, huh?

SAP AG, headquartered in Walldorf, Germany, is the supplier. The best known product is R/3, which stands for Release 3. The next major product on the horizon is R/4. This product nomenclature often leads to some head shaking. SAP spends enormous amounts of money on research and development as well as on marketing but cannot come up with the scratch to develop a name for its product that doesn't conjure memories of a Star Wars robot. R2? R3? R2D2?

The product we will be referring to through the remainder of this book is their product R/3, but most of what we have to say is entirely relevant to R/4. If you are at a point at which those distinctions matter, there are parts of this book you may wish to pass by.

Just to be clear, the world at large still refers to both the company *and* the product as SAP, as in "We decided to implement SAP because of its integrated data base."

Due to continuous upgrades, distinctions must be made between versions of R/3. These come in numeric/alpha format, such as R/3 version 3.0b.

Beyond these distinctions, there is a vast world of initial-speak in the world of SAP, beginning with the applications. Financials are referred to as Eff Eye, Sales & Distribution as Ess Dee, and Materials Management as Em Em. This is a great leap forward for those of us who only understand English. The R/2 initials for Financials are RK (from the German).

As a basic sampling:

Initial	Meaning
FI	Financials
SD	Sales & Distribution
MM	Materials Management
PP	Production Planning
HR	Human Resources

As will be seen (to the point of distraction) the applications are tightly integrated and so initials are often glued together to better define terms. Someone working in the Process Industry version of Production Planning will be referred to as a PP-PI. If you see SD-MM, you will understand that it refers the elements of Materials Management that are integrated with Sales & Distribution.

If you are an apprentice to SAP, there is no need to learn all of the initial-speak. Through the remainder of this publication, we will make every effort to spell things out. If we fail to do so and you find you are el oh ess tee, please refer to the back of the book for a complete glossary of terms.

Features of SAP, or "Why We Chose SAP" as Quoted in Countless After-the-Fact Business Articles

The allure of SAP software is not found in its business modules alone, but in its overall features. Functional comparisons of SAP to competitors such as Baan and Peoplesoft thus often lead to misconceptions because an apples-to-apples comparison of applications fails to take into account the enterprise-wide nature of SAP. Indeed, it is often said that competitors' packages for individual applications stack up nicely against SAP but, as discussed in Chapter 1, individual applications are less and less cogent to business as we know it.

In this section, we explore the operational and business features of SAP that have contributed to its phenomenal success and its status as the least understood business product of its generation.

These features are:

❑ Complete Suite of Integrated Applications

❑ Open Systems Architecture

❑ Global Business Architecture

❑ Three-Tier Client Server

❑ Transparency Between SAP and PC Applications

❑ Audit Trail and Data Integrity Controls.

❑ Connectivity

Complete Suite of Integrated Applications

This is by far the most alluring and powerful feature of SAP software and hinges on two operative elements: complete and integrated.

Numerous competitors offer integrated applications, but none compare to the vastness of SAP's list of business applications. Beyond core business functions (Finance, Sales & Distribution, Materials Management, etc.), SAP includes Plant Maintenance, Quality Maintenance, Project System, Human Resources, Production Planning, and much, much more. Further, there are industry-specific elements for oil and gas, chemicals, retail, automotive, and process manufacturing. SAP tries very hard to be all things to all companies, and although it fails to supply everything under the sun, there has been a continual flow of new applications, upgrades, and industry-specific bolt-ons.

What is fairly magical, however, is that all of these applications still work with a single, integrated data base. The significance of this feature cannot be understated.

❑ Data integrity is assured.

❑ Data handling and maintenance are vastly simplified.

❑ No interfaces are required between applications.

❑ Transactions are updated across the board on an immediate basis. Thus, management information is up-to-the-minute, not as of the last batch run.

SAP is not alone in providing real-time data updates, but it does stand alone in providing real time updating in an integrated fashion throughout a complete applications suite.

When a wing nut drops on a production line, SAP hears a ping in accounting, materials management, and possibly one or two other applications.

Open Systems Architecture

Since the beginning of cyber time, applications have been written according to the house rules as laid down by the platform on which the software will run. Each hardware vendor offers different operating systems which work with different programming languages. A company with IBM hardware that wants to purchase software that runs only on Hewlett Packard platforms will be out of luck.

Large firms which have distributed their processing across disparate sites have by and large developed heterogenous computer parks, mixing IBM with HP or DEC with NEC or Apple with Orange. (The resulting interface spaghetti need not be elaborated here.)

SAP eliminates the platform question with an open systems architecture, which functions on a number of different platforms. These include HP, IBM, Digital Equipment, Sun, and various others. Further, clients have a choice of data base systems and operating systems.

The immediate phenomenal success of R/3 would have been seriously compromised if the software was not built in such a way. Acquiring and implementing SAP software is costly enough; if clients are also required to change over entire computer parks, the pill may be too large to swallow.

The 'portability' of R/3 will also have an effect on the life cycle of your system. As your company expands or contracts, the hardware base will expand or contract, but you will be able to jiggle R/3 into any size environment without having to give it a makeover. In similar fashion, if your company expands through acquisition and the acquired firm has different hardware, R/3 can probably fold it into your organization without major new hardware expense.

Global Business Architecture

Facture, factura, rechnung, invoice. These are all the same to SAP. Though Made In Germany, the software is now fully global and is the only applications suite on the market that can make this claim.

Its global features include:

Screens and Language

The language appearing on screens, on-line help, and on-line documentation can appear in whatever language the user's log-on dictates. Obviously, not *all* languages in the universe are available. You can have English, French, German, Swedish. You cannot have Urdu, not yet. You can have Japanese, Italian, Spanish, Arabic, Dutch, Greek, and Texan. You cannot have Latin, but you can see roman numerals on occasion.

As of this writing, SAP software is said to be available in over thirty languages. Admittedly, it is more completely there for you in German and English than for some other languages since newer translations take longer to roll out, particularly for the online help. My friend James Chow tells me that much of the Mandarin Chinese is still missing, for example.

The fact that language is user-driven means that users in various countries can all be logged on at the same time, each working in their local language, using whatever parts of the system they desire. As an old story goes, an order can be entered in German in Hamburg, the materials can be ordered from Paris in French for delivery in Dutch to Brussels for manufacturing, and invoiced in English to the customer in Des Moines.

Multi-Currency and Human Resources

Beyond language, country-specific considerations are taken into account by SAP. Multiple currencies can be handled in a variety of ways (fixed rates, rates updated via external data base, average periodic rates, et al). Further, tax considerations by jurisdiction (country, province, state, NAFTA, GATT, EC) are addressed as table-driven system controls.

One long-delayed application was HR for North America, which varies radically from HR overseas. It was not until mid releases of version 3.0 of R/3 that North American HR/Payroll was truly operational. Since 1996, SAP has been pounding its competition in the world of global HR systems, all of which tend to offer only European or only North American.

Multi-Tier Architecture

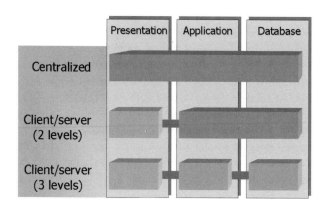

Three-Tier Client/Server

"The computer says..." is an obsolete notion as newer technology has replaced "the" computer with networks of multiple computers. In the same fashion, the work of individual computers, how they *serve*, has become more specialized and refined. There are three basic ways in which computers may serve a client:

❑ Presentation - the expression or output of information

❑ Application - the work that is accomplished

❑ Data - the supply of data used as a basis of the application

Until recent years, most computers (even in distributive environments) have been asked to perform all three services, but in multi-tier architectures the services are provided separately.

Presentation servers determine how data is viewed and manipulated. SAP offers various graphical user interfaces -GUI- the most popular of which is the Windows GUI.

A user logs on to a presentation server and can request an application, which in turn will request a needed database.

The overwhelming advantage of client/server architecture is that processing power is offered to users as they need it. This efficiency of utilization allows firms to change or "tune" their architecture according to business changes.

Another advantage of SAP in the client/server realm is that the servers do not have to be of the same make or supplier. SAP supports an impressive array of operating systems, data base systems, and GUIs.

This is largely due to Basis, a middleware between the operating system and the servers which allows for smooth operations across dif- ferent servers, operating systems, and data bases.

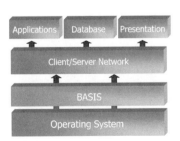

Many clients use the Unix operation system on Hewlett Packard platforms, an Oracle database, and the Windows standard

SAPGUI, but your choice will be dictated by the current state of your computer park, the ambitions you have in regard to client/server usage, and, as always, control of the purse strings.

Transparency Between SAP Applications and PC Applications

Microsoft and SAP have long been engaged in a fairly serious partnership and as the Windows standard for graphical user interface has come to dominate the world, SAP offers exceptional integration between Microsoft applications and its own applications. With the flexibility afforded by multi-tier client service, Microsoft (or other PC-based) applications can be run separately or within the context of SAP.

For example, data can be extracted with standard SAP tools and manipulated with Microsoft Excel, Word, Access, or whatever. If your firm has a Microsoft background and users are already familiar with Windows navigation and standards, SAP software will not look all that foreign to them.

Audit Trail and Data Integrity Controls

SAP software is an auditor's dream. Every transaction is logged and 'fingerprinted' as to who made the transaction (user ID), when it was made, and what it was. Further, there is no way to simply void or delete errors. Mistaken input has to be backed out of the system and error checking can include the matching of transactions that lead to an error and its subsequent resolution.

The system disciplines are rigid, which often leads people to complain about how inflexible the system can be. Sometimes this argument comes from the same people who seldom follow an agenda during meetings, push on doors marked 'pull', and never order what's on the menu when they go to restaurants. However, as Nancy Bancroft points out, "the system's rigid structure imposes some difficulty on those trying to configure it to meet their requirements. I also find that this structure, while useful to many, can provide an environment that just does not suit some company cultures."

In essence, system disciplines and rigidity can be traced to the integrated nature of the software and the inadvisability of customizing it through ABAP programming. In traditional IS, you can throw a team of programmers at an application till it fits your organization like a glove. You will find that R/3 is occasionally a mitten and the lack of dexterity can be frustrating.

Connectivity

Computer to computer communications have increased a thousandfold in the 1990's and SAP provides multiple manners for getting connected. The three most common modes for communication and connection are:

❏ ALE: Application Link Enabling

❏ EDI: Electronic Data Interchange

❏ The Internet.

ALE - Application Link Enabling

This technology is a slick version of interfacing, in which applications from disparate systems are linked where needed. Often, the links are R/3 to R/3 (for companies with multiple installations), but it is also possible to use ALE for links to other systems.

EDI - Electronic Data Interchange

Until recently, the electronic exchange of data between business entities was limited to bank transfers and various other financial applications. With the development of international data standards and the arrival of object-oriented technology, electronic data interchange has been expanded to include the exchange of commercial data as well.

With EDI, SAP users can exchange data with clients and suppliers, whether or not they also have SAP installations. The EDI interface can trigger functions within SAP applications for instant processing or hold incoming data for manual processing that requires human intervention.

EDI is not an area for business people. This is still a technical arena and requires people with a knowledge of data base, telecommunications protocols, and usually a bit of ABAP/4.

The Internet

Ma Bell was broken up in the early 1980's, but in France the PTT has maintained its telecommunications monopoly. As such, it was able to introduce the Minitel in 1983. This consisted of a small terminal that could be connected to any telephone and allowed for telecom connections to computer networks. Unsurprisingly, the popular 'engine' behind early Minitel use were the sexual connections (what was referred to as the 'Minitel Rose') but inevitably business applications were introduced. With the Minitel, clients could dial up suppliers' applications and direct enter orders, query existing orders, or leave a Minitel version of e-mail. Suppliers could inform clients of impending deliveries or delays. Banking data was made available to depositors and investors and the notion of the 'home' computer reached fruition as the Minitel also allowed for home banking, travel reservations, information bases, a form of e-mail, and 'online' games.

The Minitel had its limitations, of course, most especially in that its use was limited to France. But if the rest of this scenario is familiar to you, consider the business possibilities of the Internet when conjoined with an SAP installation.

Since version 3.1, R/3 is Internet-ready. The enormous possibilities offered by the Internet are highlighted by the fact that:

⏌ Business processes are extended beyond the "borders" of enterprises.

⏌ With Internet browser use, no training is required and the customer base is widened to a worldwide proportion.

⏌ Business can be conducted 24 hours a day, 365 days a year.

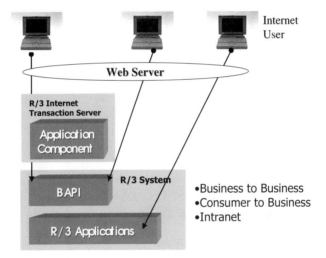

For instance, Chrysler is said to be developing a client/server application called "Selling Chain" that will integrate with SAP and allow customers to shop for new cars via the Internet or at freestanding kiosks. Customers will be able to 'design' their new car by keying in specific information from a menu of choices, i.e. color, add-ons, safety features, payment limits, etc. Online price quotes will also be offered. In practice, Chrysler will be in a position to deliver exactly what the customer wants, and also receive direct data on which to base its monthly production planning.

Internet applications may be business to business, consumer to business, business to financial institutions, or a combination of SAP R/3 and Intranet.

In a world in which competition and cooperation have settled into co-opetition, the use of Extra-nets is more and more widespread. Extra-nets are the connections between one or more firms' Intranets (or company-only Internets). Extra-nets allow for a pooling of software, direct communications (at Internet low rates) and a people-less flow of data that can be beneficial to all parties.

SAP allows for business-to-business Internet as well as Extra-net and any firm that is moving to R/3 is well advised to explore these possibilities up front. It is safe to say that every firm is already directly affected by these e-developments in an ever more e-world. It is amazing to find how many firms are still without even rudimentary web sites. These are the firms that you might find in the Yellow Pages. You remember the Yellow Pages. You remember Nehru jackets, too. And you love the movie 'Grease'. And the phone still rings. Sometimes.

The technology for connectivity is there and the possibilities are breathtaking if you consider the elements of access that the Internet provides.

Of Screen Doors, Babel, and Healthy Paranoia

When it comes to the Internet, access and reliability are among the chief concerns of SAP users, with good reason. Once you have opened your systems to global access, it is as though you have opened a window into your own home, an aperture that will attract bugs (viruses) and crawling critters (hackers). What you need to protect your site is a screen door and it happens that an increasing variety of security services are already in place.

In addition, the global aspect of the Internet is often overstated. More than eighty percent of Internet users worldwide can be found in North America and restrictions on Internet use vary according to democratic levels and degrees of state paranoia.

For example, in 1995 Hong Kong police disconnected all but one of the colony's Internet providers in search of a hacker. Ten thousand people were left without Net access. (source: API)

A Human Rights Watch has reported:

China requires users and ISPs to register with the police. Germany once cut off access to some newsgroups carried on Compuserve. In Saudi Arabia, Internet access has been confined to universities and hospitals. Singapore requires political and religious content providers to register with the state. New Zealand classifies computer disks as "publications" that can be censored and seized.

Internet troubles are not confined to overseas sites. In July of 1995, thousands in Minneapolis-St. Paul lost Net access after transients started a bonfire under a bridge at the University of Minnesota causing fiber-optic cables to melt (source: API).

These sorts of interruptions should not overly concern you for domestic business to business connections, but should be taken into consideration for global Internet use.

Core Business Applications of SAP

We will first zoom in on the hardy perennials, the absolute core of the applications suite, and then some of the other key applications (referred to herein as Workflow applications) and focus solely on the characteristics and features important to management.

The core business applications offered by SAP are the same as those offered (individually, in most cases) by traditional package software vendors: Finance, Controlling, Sales & Distribution, Materials Management, Production Planning, and Human Resources. Since the arrival of R/3, the Financials (FI) have had a solid reputation of being at the top of the charts in the world of software, most often cited as being the equal of, say, Dun & Bradstreet. The Sales & Distribution (SD) module is often criticized as "heavy" and difficult to master. This is because R/3 is one product intended to serve diverse masters. Sales and distribution vary widely between retail, build-to-order, manufacturing, health, banking, and other industries. Such diversity has its natural consequences to Materials Management (MM) and Production Planning (PP) as industry-specific considerations require SAP to dance with several feet at once. When you seek implementation, there is at first a tangle of sorts that SAP unravels, with varying success, through its industry-specific templates and aids.

Human Resources is the latecomer to this suite. Until 1996, the missing piece was North American payroll, which is far different from the European payroll method that was used as the initial basis. The notion of Human Resources as a whole varies from country to country and SAP was further hard-pressed to satisfy differing philosophies regarding unions, employment rights, and working conditions.

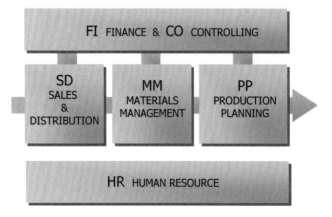

Few companies implement much more than these core applications first. Most begin with FI and then carry on. Others implement all of these core applications in one go. Still other companies implement *some* of these core applications and *interface* them to legacy systems, which makes little sense but adds a mountain of consulting hours and keeps people busy.

Workflow Applications

Plant Maintenance, Project Systems, Workflow, and Quality Maintenance represent a second tier of SAP modules. Whereas Plant Maintenance is more of a functional application, the others relate directly to the flow of work throughout an enterprise.

Plant Maintenance and Quality Maintenance are just what they are named. Each has industry-specific wrinkles and are tightly integrated with Production Planning and, to some degree, with Materials Management.

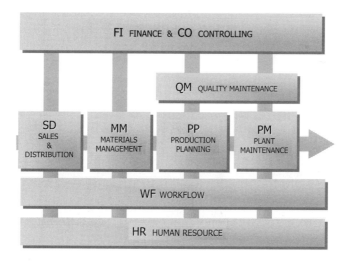

The Workflow module allows for an automation of business processes, combining human and computer 'events' or activities which trigger one another to the conclusion of a process. After basic business process reengineering (that box-arrow-box exercise), the system can be configured to address horizontal business flow. However, Workflow takes this a step further by automating the process. Each event or activity is assigned to a person or the system, its duration is fixed, and work that is relative to a defined process is routed throughout an organization.

Until the past few years, few clients had much experience with these modules. It was enough to get the core modules up and running. Therefore, finding experienced consulting help or reference sites for these modules is more difficult.

EIS - Executive Information System

Managers crave information, but they do not always crave the same information. The failure of most MIS systems is that they offer periodic, fixed reports, but the value of established reports fades within a very short time because, while business marches on, the reports do not. Information, not reports, is what is asked for.

SAP offers a tool for the development of a parallel data base that can be used for ad hoc report generation by senior management. In principle, the data that will be afforded as the result of an EIS will be "information" by virtue of the variety of ways the data can be easily manipulated (sorted) and expressed (in tables, data lists, spreadsheets, or graphics). As your R/3 installation changes through time, the data base at the source of the EIS will also be changed, so the information will continue to be available despite changes to the base system.

It all sounds dreamy, but the reporting of information is a sore point when it comes to any business systems support. To executives, systems supports are usually judged primarily on the merits of their ability to provide "information". In this same light, it is often the executives who should be judged.

There is something that the nerds understand quite well and have been at pains for years to express to the business people, and that is the twin concepts of data integrity and how data becomes information. Constantly faced with a bewildering array of decisions to be made, executives often seek to surround themselves with data that will either guide or justify a decision. Whereas information is considered a most valuable commodity, we are often at loose ends about what information is useful, what information is anecdotal, and what information is an alibi.

In an installment of Peanuts, Lucy recounts a series of damning pitching statistics to Charlie Brown, who replies: "Tell your statistics to shut up." How many times have we felt the same need?

Having said all this, we do believe that EIS will bring some benefit to your project: its inclusion will help you gain project support from senior executives.

SE: Will I get all my reports?

You: You betcha.

SE: I'm in. Where do I sign?

ABAP/4 Development Workbench

Software companies like the term 'workbench' and we can imagine that their marketing teams like it as well. The term evokes a sense of concrete labor and the promise of results. SAP follows suit, and also applies it to the "Business Engineering

Workbench", which is really no workbench at all, just a collection of aids and tools for business process reengineering.

However, the ABAP/4 Development Workbench is the real deal. It is a set of related tools for the development of new applications or the enhancement of existing SAP applications. This workbench includes:

- Editor
- Screen and Menu Painters
- Interactive Debugger
- Computer-aided test tools
- Development tools using dynpro technology
- ABAP/4 Dictionary
- Enterprise data model

SAP's products are written in ABAP/4, a language developed and enhanced by SAP itself. It is a fourth generation language, relatively easy to learn, and the workbench provides solid support to the ABAPers who will be needed on occasion for R/3 customization.

And All the Rest

Having offered a cursory overview of the company and the features and applications of R/3, we cannot state that we have told you what SAP is. In both breadth of scope and depth of functionality, the software is seemingly boundless and SAP itself offers fat 9"x12" color-coded volumes for each of the applications.

We have not yet mentioned Assets Management, Inventory Management, Warehouse Management, or Service Management, nor have we mentioned that the upcoming Version 4.0 of R/3 will offer solid functionality for retail applications...

Beyond these subjects, there are report and query aids,

SAPScript, Data Warehousing, Business Engineering Workbench, Early Watch Program, Team SAP, Accelerated SAP, and more. But this is a concise business guide, not an exhaustive technical text, so let us simply carry on in that vein, confident that the SAP pool is far deeper than this chapter cares to say.

Critical Distinctions Between SAP and What You Know

When in the field, consultants tend to repeat certain phrases over and over. Often, these repetitions include sighs of exasperation, but the phrases must be repeated time and again because of the distinctions between SAP and what you have known in the past.

Among these phrases are:

"SAP is a business project, not an IS project"

"We're not programming here, we're configuring"

"It's integrated software, so what you do in (fill in department name) will immediately affect (fill in department name)"

Often, the difficulty in getting key messages across lies with the experience of the audience. Nearly everyone involved in an SAP implementation has already participated in at least one traditional IS project and will tend to rely upon that experience as instructive. It may well be, but only partially so.

Do not entrench yourself into a Maginot Line of past experience and how you won the last war. In order to accelerate a conversion to SAP thinking, you should absorb and retain the lessons of this chapter, which will take a great strain off both yourselves and your consultants.

CRITICAL DISTINCTION #1:
SAP is a Business Endeavor, Not a Computer Endeavor

As elaborated in the first chapter, business folks are no longer the hostages of computer technology. In this light, there are multiple distinctions between SAP and what you know.

The first is that business people not only determine what the systems should do, but they also directly bend existing software to their wills. This is done by configuring R/3 according to established rules and methods.

The distinction between programming and configuring is of huge import. Programming requires 'technical' knowledge. Configuring requires 'business' knowledge.

Configuring is the setting of business tables that determine the format, the nature, the location, and the destination of information.

Programming is the creation of codes that manipulate the format, the nature, the location, and the destination of information.

Which of these do you find more understandable?

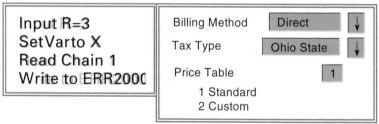

In essence, R/3 is comprised of hundreds of tables like that on the right, all of which drive data according to the rules laid down by business people.

This leads to a second sub-distinction, which is the disappearance of the traditional negotiation between business and IS groups for new information services or changes to existing services. In sum, R/3 is business software for business people, created by business people, and maintained by business people as business evolves.

This phrase could be a bumper sticker.

CRITICAL DISTINCTION # 2:
Integration = Enterprise-wide = Horizontal Processes

Your project will not succeed if you think of separately building individual applications in the way you have in the past. Decisions that you make about Materials Management will certainly have repercussions in Sales & Distribution and Financials, and possibly in Production Planning.

Further, your core implementation will take you longer than would the implementation of a new accounting package or a customized sales order processing module. Remember, you are not simply installing software, you are re-inventing the manner in which your company functions. Thus, your implementation team will be comprised of representatives from throughout the company and each will be tempted to defend the turf of his or her current domain. Turf protection is harmful to enterprise-wide thinking. In these matters, "Let's get horizontal" has a whole new meaning.

Says Nancy Bancroft, "I have found that because SAP is so integrated, the system produces immediate visibility of departmental information. This is another reason for up-front emphasis on BPR, management education, and coalition building. Finance will see when Manufacturing has an overrun *as soon as Manufacturing sees it.* This visibility of data is a sword that cuts both ways."

Another factor of an enterprise-wide undertaking is *the heightening of risk*. The stakes are higher, the potential benefits more dramatic, and the costs more visible than for a traditional systems undertaking. A lot of nervous activity occurs in such an environment. Emotions are jangled and tempers are tested. This is why change management is a subset of SAP projects. (More on this to come.)

CRITICAL DISTINCTION #3:
Integration Places an Added Burden on Direct Users

One of the prime sources of resistance to an SAP implementation is the direct (or end) user group. This resistance is often related to a simple fear of change or a loathing to learn another system. This much can be overcome with good project leadership, but another cause for resistance to SAP is the added burden that it places on such users. This burden takes two forms:

Time: Compared to most legacy systems, R/3 requires more input and more complex input for the majority of its functions. Users will rightfully complain that for R/3 they are forced to use three different screens to fulfill a function that required only a single screen for legacy systems.

Authority/Responsibility: Workflow eliminates a major portion of supervisory tasks and the integrated nature of R/3 puts power into the hands of the users. The entry of data is no longer simply a chore of reporting to the system but is now an instigator of action. Someone entering even supplementary data to an existing sales order is virtually working for accounting (cash flow), materials management (requisition), and production planning (for manufacturing and delivery dates) all at the same time. Sniff the air and it smells of empowerment; not that Dilbertville bogus empowerment, but the real thing.

CRITICAL DISTINCTION #4:
The System Life Cycle is Vastly Extended

No longer will you have to envision replacing your software wholesale or in large segments every five years or so. (For more on this subject, see the first section of Chapter 3: SAP in a Microwave).

SAP is the On-Ramp; Workflow is the Highway

As we reach into the next millenium, IS technologies are melding sweetly with telecommunications and, just as important, with new business vistas that are a radical departure from the norms that have been in place since the end of World War II. One foundation of these norms is a compartmentalization of business functions. We have had sales departments, accounting departments, stock departments, shipping departments...and various other labels for the business tribes that fulfill specific piecemeal functions within an enterprise. This notion has been tinkered with in various ways, like the creation of customer service departments in which sales, stock, and deliveries have been melded, or Just in Time logistics methods which have replaced the need for so many depots. Still, the model has been one in which a 'sale' is passed from marketing (pre-sales) to sales (the order) to purchasing (raw materials) to production (manufacture) to deliveries (packing) to accounting (invoice and

Information Systems

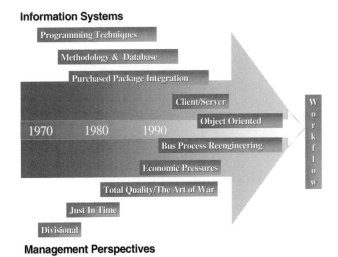

Management Perspectives

collection) and various other skeins in similar networks. These hand-offs take time, reduce accountability, and worse, in systems terms, usually require interfaces.

Over the past fifteen years, the face of business has changed enormously with increasing client pressure for faster service, wider choices, and ever lower prices. The globalization of business has accelerated in this same time period and organizations have been redrawn as a result. Yet for each of the from-to's noted in the preceding paragraph, businesses have traditionally had a different applications system and these systems have been strung together with the sputtering, blinking Christmas lights known as interfacing. And with each change in business conditions, each management initiative, systems people are obliged to update not only the applications systems but also all affected interfaces. How have systems folks kept up with it? Quite simply, they have not kept up.

> Workflow is the procedural automation of a business process through the ordering of work activities intended to support a business strategy.

An old programming dictum goes as follows:

> Perfection has been reached not when there is nothing left to add, but when there is nothing left to take away

Sloppy programmers (or those with deadline gun barrels at their temples) tend to use more instructions, loops, lines of code, and jumps than do slick, spartan programmers.

This same principle is at the heart of the notion of workflow, which is intended to alter the way we have worked since roughly the second world war.

To paraphrase the programming dictum:

> Workflow reaches its profitable peak not when there is nothing

left to add, but when there is nothing left to take away.

Definitions of workflow abound. For the purposes of this exercise, our definition is:

Workflow is the procedural automation of a business process through the ordering of work activities intended to support a business strategy.

The notion of workflow erases the old notion of compartmentalization. To appreciate what workflow brings to an organization requires a radical shift in your point of view. A firm's responsibility (or mission) is to serve its clientele. Compartmentalized business allows for successful surgery ("the marketing worked and orders are pouring in!") while allowing the patient to die ("the raw materials arrived too late and we couldn't manufacture in time so the order was cancelled"). Workflow assigns responsibility, oversight, and control through entire business processes. For example, order fulfillment, as a *business process*, covers the entire horizontal spectrum from marketing to invoice & collection.

Think of the Panama Canal in which a ship has to pass through series of locks or segments. Flow is interrupted at each gate; waiting is a part of the deal...lag time. This is the business you are currently dealing in, in which the vessel of each deal bumps from lock to lock, department to department, hand to hand, until the client has his M&Ms and you have your cash. Workflow means that there are no locks or segments. It means that the vessel flows freely from point A (the client wants something from you) to point B (the client has what he wants and you have the cash in return). Smooth.

The bottom line is that when business processes lead to workflow, key areas of the company that were once only in the domain of research and development are now distributed throughout the enterprise:

⌐ The improvement of a process or a service
⌐ The development of a new product
⌐ The reduction of labor.

All businesses are compartmentalized to one degree or another. It is business tradition. For workflow to exist, a firm must reengineer its business processes and replace the vertical step-handoff-step routine with horizontal business processes. This much is now clear to nearly everyone, but information systems that rely upon interfaces cannot support workflow. This is where SAP comes in.

By providing a complete suite of integrated applications as well as a specific Workflow module, SAP *enables* workflow, and workflow is the primary source of the benefits you seek. A simple installation of SAP software may not save your company a dime. Think of SAP as a pier. It will only get you halfway across the river. Building a complete bridge is a project team's preliminary challenge. Crossing that bridge is, ultimately, a management challenge.

The Order Fulfillment Process

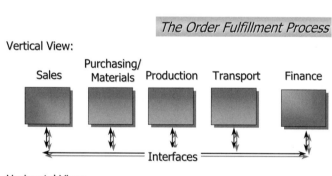

Vertical View:

Integrated suite of applications = no interfaces

Order Fulfillment: A Simple Example of Major Process Simplifications

AS-IS

	Activity	Time	Lag	Cum
1	Phone order	0.1	0.1	
2	Entry into system	0.1	0.2	0.3
3	Verification/acknowled	0.1	1.0	1.3
4	Purchase order-mat.	0.2	3.0	4.3
5	Receive materials	0.1	6.0	10.3
6	Production	2.0	10.0	20.3
7	Packing	0.1	1.0	21.3
8	Shipment	0.1	0.0	21.3
9	Invoicing	0.1	2.0	23.3

	Time	Lag	
Total	2.9	23.3	
Nbr of Orders	300		
	Time	Lag	
Total workload	870	23.3	

An existing Order Fulfillment Process, in which phone orders are taken manually and later entered into the system.

Interfaces between sales and production systems account for the lag at the purchase order step.

The total turnaround for each order is 2.9 days with an average span/lag of 23.3 days from receipt of the order to the issuance of an invoice.

TO BE (A)

	Activity	Time	Lag	Cum
1	EDI from client	0.0	0.0	
2	Purchase order-	0.2	3.0	3.0
3	Verify purchases	0.1	1.0	4.0
4	Receive Materials	0.1	6.0	10.0
5	Production	2.0	10.0	20.0
6	Packing	0.1	1.0	21.0
7	Shipment/Invoice	0.1	0.0	21.0

Total	2.6	21.0	
Nbr of Orders	300		
Total workload	780	21.0	
Monthly gain (hours)	90		
Gain per order	0.3	2.3	days

Electronic data interchange is used so that client orders are automatically updated to the system.

The invoicing is transferred from accounting and incorporated in the shipping sub-process.

A gain of .3 days of labor and 2.3 days' reduction in order fulfillment turnaround is realized.

TO BE (B)

	Activity	Time	Lag	Cum
1	EDI from client	0.0	0.0	
2	EDI purchase	0.0	0.0	
3	Verify purchases	0.1	1.0	1.0
4	Receive Materials	0.1	6.0	7.0
5	Production	2.0	10.0	17.0
6	Packing	0.1	1.0	18.0
7	Shipment/Invoice	0.1	0.0	18.0

Total	2.4	18.0	
Nbr of Orders	300		
Total workload	720	18.0	
Monthly gain (hours)	150		
Gain per order	0.5	5.3	days

EDI is also used for standard purchases based upon incoming sales orders.

Another 3 lag days are eliminated from the turnaround time, as well as .5 days of labor. The integration of sales and purchasing also reduces the lag time.

The gain to the company is 150 hours of labor with a slicing of 5.3 days from turnaround.

CHAPTER 3

SAP in a Microwave

⏌ A New System Life Cycle

⏌ SAP in a Micro-wave

⏌ Post Implementation: The Windfall

⏌ One Size Fits All (With Reservations)

⏌ Certified Business Solutions

⏌ How Rapid SAP R/3 Implementation Methods Can Be Misleading

SAP in a Microwave

A New System Life Cycle: Continuous Business Improvement

One of the pre-eminent challenges for information systems people has traditionally been the prolongation of the useful life of an implemented system. "Useful life" may have a malleable definition, but should

> It isn't over till it's over.
> Yogi Berra

generally be viewed as "serving the base requirements of the company" (minimum) to "providing business impetus, direction, and economy" (paradigm).

Major IS investments are often followed by major upheavals in a business climate and systems have seldom been updated or enhanced to reflect those upheavals. Thus, the speed of degradation of performance has increased as business complexity has increased.

The life cycle of an information system has traditionally been viewed as circular, as illustrated in the upcoming chart.

In most projects, the degradation of usefulness begins during the acquisition/development stage. The lag time between project planning (during which goals and objectives are established) and implementation can be anywhere from three to twelve months, during which time the business environment will have changed, sometimes radically. Project scope is seldom updated to address those changes and the implemented systems tend to be a source of disappointment.

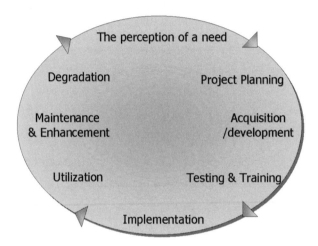

A second, continual phase of degradation begins once the implementation is completed and the system is moved into maintenance mode. Programming alone cannot keep pace with business changes (and consequent changes in needs), most especially because the business changes in question will have an impact on system architecture and interfacing. The IS burden is therefore complicated by functional requirements, integration requirements, and information requirements. It is not surprising that traditional IS cannot meet these expectations.

Degradation occurs when information systems no longer match company needs. Needs change as business changes. And needs can scarcely be met with traditional IS methods.

With SAP, however, this life cycle does not have to be followed. Instead, a cycle of continuous business improvement can be envisioned in that the SAP infrastructure can be modified by business people according to business changes *as they occur* with considerably less delay and disappointment.

Once SAP is implemented, the system should no longer follow this pattern. Add-on modules and upgrades will always be needed, just as there will also be a "wish list" of functionality that could not be implemented in the core project.

For the core of your business (and a large core at that) you should not find it necessary to redesign or replace software. As needs arise and the performance of the system is found wanting, your company may find it advantageous to re-engineer the business processes that were the model of the initial implementation and reflect changes in the SAP configuration.

Continuous Business Improvement Cycle

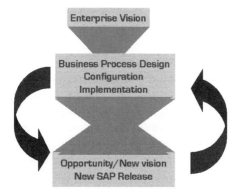

This should best be a continuous process just as *business is a continuous process.* Many firms make the mistake of implementing

SAP, throwing a Friday night party, (oh those wild SAP parties!) and then stopping on Monday, on the faulty assumption that they now have all they need in the world of information systems. Once implementation is complete, teams are disbanded and SAP efforts are converted into maintenance. This maintenance mentality should be avoided at all costs. SAP should not be maintained like some Cobol-based information system. It should continue to evolve *just as your business evolves*, in the same fashion, at the same pace. Company reorganizations, the incorporation of new distribution methods, emerging markets, acquisitions and mergers, all have an effect on the information system. As configurable software, SAP allows for a rapid response to changes in business climate and degradation of information services should not occur.

Adds Nancy Bancroft, "I think the issue is greater than the life cycle. I think it is a matter of how a company *thinks about* their systems. Companies that implement an integrated system successfully approach the task with a more comprehensive viewpoint than ever before. They understand the need to balance the technical, workflow, business, and worker concerns. Of course, plenty of companies don't do this with a corresponding lessening of bang for their buck."

The term 'implementation' can be misleading. In traditional systems projects, the implementation was the end point in which the new system began to function in place of the old and thereafter only maintenance and enhancements were required. However, an SAP endeavor, embracing business process reengineering and the installation of integrated enterprise-wide software should necessarily lead to a new life cycle in which continuous reengineering will take place.

In this chapter, we are addressing what should be referred to as 'core implementation'; that is, the first implementation of base modules required to support your business. Whether this is a phased (or rollout) implementation, in which modules or business sectors are put in play sequentially or a big bang (all modules at the same time) is of no import. The point that must be made is that true implementation is no longer finite but core implementation is.

SAP in a Microwave

The following is not a complete guide for implementation, merely a rapid tour of how a successful implementation will proceed. For the purposes of this exercise, we will stick primarily to the critical path of an SAP implementation project. The education/change management track is addressed elsewhere in this book and the technical track is not what this book is about.

As we have pointed out numerous times, SAP ventures do not follow traditional paths. However, in terms of a core implementation, the traditional Planning, Development, and Conversion stages still apply.

The Planning Stage

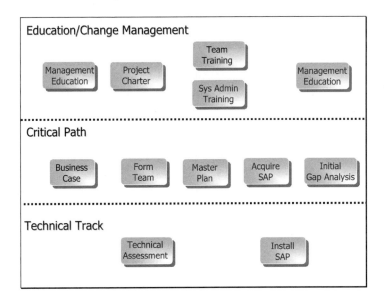

The planning stage can be subdivided into these phases:

⌐ Envision the Future

⌐ Plan the Venture

⌐ Gather the Elements.

Phase 1: Envision the Future

At the onset of your endeavor, you should envision the future, justify the means to that future with a business case, and express the vision and the means to project members and employees with a project charter.

We will assume that you have sufficient strategic forces at your disposal to adequately fulfill this task and our purpose here is not to provide guidance for strategic planning. However, one caution begs inclusion: do not let your vision become polluted with mission statements or simple slogans. If you are seeking to trim costs (and headcount) while vastly improving your production and positioning yourselves to take advantage of emerging markets, say so. Use tangible terms, not jingoism, or your employee body will doubt the purpose behind the endeavor and your resistance level will be dangerously high.

Business Case

Justifying the cost of business systems projects is usually a discomfiting, paper-driven affair in which various individuals are asked to list intended benefits and a clever soul from accounting will gather it all together and pin dollar figures to each of them.

The task here is a cost-benefit analysis and once you have estimated the costs of the project, you should be able to compare them to tangible, measurable benefits as well as those hard-to-define gains, like "improved communications." The business case is a dollars exercise and should provide the financial measuring stick for success or failure.

This business case should address:

⏢ description of the mission (why it is being undertaken and what is the intended result)
⏢ project context and priority
⏢ anticipated hard benefits and rate of return
⏢ anticipated soft benefits and schedule of return
⏢ an assessment of the potential impact on current business for the duration of the project.

Project Charter

One of the greatest impediments to success in implementing R/3 is the rumor mill. Employees catch wind that an implementation is imminent and a man says he hears it includes "some serious restructuring" and one woman remembers reading about how SAP is a corporate downsizing tool, and another was once in a company that implemented R/3 and oh, boy there were wall-to-wall consultants.

You get the idea.

You can move ahead of the rumor mill and stay comfortably ahead of it by developing a Project Charter (based upon the Vision and the Business Case) that will serve as the enterprise definition of the project, stating its aims in an unambiguous and, yes, inspirational manner.

This charter should be signed by the CEO and any members of senior management who are fulfilling the role of project sponsor. It should then be distributed to all employees at the onset of the project. In succeeding months, news of the project (in newsletters, town hall meetings, etc.) should refer to this document and the vision therein to allow for a clear communication of project progress.

Points to be addressed in a Project Charter:

- ⌐ the name of the project (slogan optional)
- ⌐ the general aims of the project
- ⌐ what business entities are involved
- ⌐ (optional) a master chart illustrating the new enterprise
- ⌐ the time frame of the project
- ⌐ who will be involved - team chart
- ⌐ why SAP was chosen
- ⌐ how this will affect the employee populace
- ⌐ a reminder of past successes.

Phase 2: Plan the Venture

Because of the new system life cycle, the planning of an SAP R/3 implementation should extend beyond the Day One of system use and should allow for the creation of an organization that will support the new infrastructure and take advantage of the considerable benefits it will afford.

If you are using the Accelerated SAP method, a template master plan is already at your disposal. (Note that business process reengineering is not an element of ASAP and you will have to amend the plan to address it. More on this later in the chapter.)

If you are not using the Accelerated SAP method, you should use planning software of some kind and take inspiration from plans that have already been used for SAP implementations. Do not use planning templates for traditional IS implementations. They will only lead you astray.

Refine and revise the plan at various points throughout the project, especially if you are working in a large organization and/or if the project duration exceeds six months. No matter how efficient the team proves to be, by the third month of any project, circumstances will have changed. Plowing ahead *as planned* is not always wise.

Most important of all, plan with realism in mind. Project plans that are molded more by company attitudes and good intentions result in projects that are 'late' and 'over budget'. Projects planned according to realistic assumptions tend to come in under both time and budgetary wires.

Betty Costa is a Senior Manager with Grant Thornton LLP and has over eight years of experience in SAP implementation project management. Her bottom line on planning is: "The SAP implementation – It's like crossing the Atlantic in a rowboat, rather than a well-equipped watercraft with the proper provisions – it's a matter of planning for the established goal. Here "planning" refers to the strength of the company executives and the assigned project managers to set the direction and stay on track. The "goal" defines the level of expectation, which the organization must maintain throughout the project, and meet at the end of the journey."

Phase 3: Gather the Elements

With a Project Charter and a Master Plan in hand, you are now prepared to form your team and acquire and install SAP R/3.

Form Your Team

The four elements of an R/3 implementation team are:

⌐ Project Management
⌐ Internal consulting
⌐ External consulting
⌐ Technical support.

Of these elements, **project management** is the most important because the other elements will reflect the manager's vision and expertise. Your firm should name a project manager who possesses a broad understanding of your business (along the horizontal plane) and support this manager with a steering committee or a sponsor from the ranks of senior management.

When an external consulting group is chosen, there will probably also be a project manager included in the mix. Many companies have been successful pairing an internal project manager with an external project manager, whose role is to guide the project through planning and the bulk of development and then turn over the keys to the client. Even if the external project manager is not assigned full-time, it is wise to have someone your project manager can rely upon for guidance.

Says Betty Costa, "This internal project manager must possess a key ingredient for success – respect within his/her organization. If you blend this with solid leadership skills, you have created the potential to more readily gain the trust and confidence of the greater business community. This individual must convince the organization at-large to believe in the new vision. Every SAP implementation needs two critical project team members: **The evangelist**: To spread the gospel of the new, transforming organization and win over the hearts and souls of all. **The psychologist**: To fix the minds of those resisters, and make them believers."

Jon Reed of Allen Davis & Associates adds, "I think this pairing strategy is often the best way to go: a project manager with 'been there, done that' SAP experience and an insider who knows the firm and can ensure the cooperation of colleagues."

For implementations of a long duration, it is normal for some of the team members to leave before the job is done. It can be disastrous if the project manager is among them, so seek to name someone whose presence can be confirmed.

A team of **internal consultants** should be drawn from your ranks and assigned full-time to the project. In smaller firms, this cannot always be accomplished so the project plan must take part-timers into account.

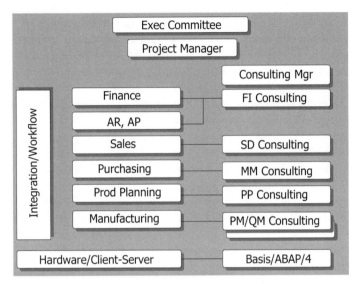

David Chapman of Lyondell-Citgo stresses that a smaller core team with widespread enterprise participation is better than a large core team and little participation. "It is not just a matter of an implementation team 'doing it' and then letting the others in on it. There is a change in depth and breadth, a change of behavior and a change of roles throughout the enterprise. If you cannot foresee acceptance of this across the company body, you might be better off postponing anything more than incremental steps".

As an example, here is how David tackled one of the thornier issues of an implementation project, namely, master data:

"Our core team built a data model for the materials master and then presented it to the materials process owners for their participation, approval, and inheritance of succeeding steps to build it. The model was accompanied by a plan and schedule for the creation of the master data and the offer of training to whoever the process owners nominated."

In short, Lyondell Citgo staff included staff outside of the 'implementing team'. Such inclusion is crucial or the project will become marginalized. 'If you build it, they will come' is not always applicable to an R/3 core implementation.

The internal team will be matched with the **external consulting** group for development and implementation of the R/3 modules chosen. The ratio of internal to external staff will depend upon the quality of staff you assign internally. If you are just grabbing available bodies, you will need more external consultants. If you assign the best and the brightest, you can lower the external consulting level, and if you also accent the transfer of SAP knowledge, you can reduce the duration of the external consultants' stay.

Jon Reed's SAP recruiting perspective: "SAP consultants with outstanding communications skills as well as strong technical or functional skills tend to be expensive, but pay for themselves by finding a way to 'duplicate' their talents on the project. So called 'soft skills' do matter."

The criteria for choosing external consultants will be covered in Chapter 4: *The Wild West of SAP Consulting*. Your choice of internal consultants will hinge upon your ability to 'sacrifice' good people to the project. This can be painful and will clearly have an impact on current business. Further, when the assignments are made, think of them as permanent. You cannot assume that at the conclusion of a core implementation that a) the people assigned will wish to return to their old jobs, b) that their old jobs will still exist, or c) that they will still be in your company.

On this last point, be aware that the long-standing shortage of SAP consultants means that you will certainly lose some of the staff that you assign to the world of consulting. The lure of six-figure salaries is often more powerful than whatever inducements you can offer to retain them.

Nancy Bancroft has had the opportunity to study this problem at a number of firms. "There are a number of steps that can be taken to reduce losses of key individuals. Successful companies have addressed this problem relatively well. Others just bite the bullet and rehire. Of course milestone bonuses and key-skill incentives are important; however promotions and an emphasis on lifestyle also help keep employees. Not everyone wants to travel all the time; some people prefer to watch their kids grow up."

Some firms have gone to odd lengths to assure retention of SAP staff by assigning only people over fifty (on the premise that they will be less inclined to embark on a new, travel-heavy, career) or by getting waivers by which employees who leave within a given period must re-imburse the firm for all SAP training they have received.

Though losses vary, experience shows that a firm will lose about a third of its internal SAP consulting staff after a year has passed. This is clearly hard to swallow and you should do what you can to minimize these losses, but the best that can be hoped for is that the staff will remain intact at least through core implementation.

Your **technical support** staff will be a combination of your existing IS group and some outside help for Basis tuning and administration and, possibly, some ABAP/4 programming. The level of support you require will correlate to the number of legacy systems you feel the urge to retain (i.e. interfacing), how much add-on programming you have put onto the menu, and the number of operational sites you are dealing with. Your IS staff will already be skittish about a conversion to SAP, so this may be a sore point. Either your RPGIII programmers are bailing out or they are asking for ABAP/4 training.

Acquire and Install SAP R/3

Until 1997, R/3 was considered to be one product that could be configured in multiple ways in order to match client needs. 1997 saw releases and announcements that have rendered multiple versions of R/3 and pre-acquisition analysis has become more complicated than before. The upside to this complication is that there are industry-specific attributes that make the product all the more attractive.

Your SAP rep will help you somewhat in choosing what to license, but you may find more knowledgeable assistance through SAP's Industry Centers of Expertise (ICOE). Centers exist for:

Consumer Packaged Goods	Process Industries
High Tech Electronics	Utilities & Communications
Financial Services	Health Care

It would also be wise to hire a solid Basis consultant to assist you in an assessment of your needs before you start ordering hardware. The platform suppliers will have some Basis background, but you would do better to have a third party advising you.

Do not delay overmuch your acquisition and installation. While this occurs, your project team should be off educating themselves to R/3. Upon their return, they will be better served if an R/3 instance is available to them.

At the conclusion of this stage, your staff will have acquired considerable SAP knowledge and you will notice that R/3 will not perform every business function that you require. Consider the shortfall to be a 'Preliminary Gap Analysis', but do not leap to fill those gaps with either additional software acquisition or plans for ABAP/4 add-on programming. Many of these perceived gaps will prove to be illusory as the project progresses and your knowledge of R/3 deepens.

The Development Stage

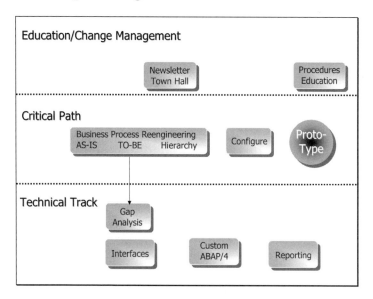

The development stage can be subdivided into three phases:

⌟ Refining the Vision

⌟ Configuring to Prototype

⌟ Technical Development.

Phase 1: Refining the Vision

The project charter offers headlines, but you will need more details before pouring your efforts into configuring R/3 to 'meet the vision'.

Refining the vision is a major step in business processing reengineering. The degree to which you wish to reengineer your enterprise will determine the complexity and duration of this phase. Will you radically change your ways or will change be more gradual?

Years ago, Calvin Griffith, at the time the owner of the Minnesota Twins, opposed the dramatic rise in baseball salaries by shuffling established stars off to other teams and bringing up newer, rawer, cheaper talent from the minor leagues. His method of tinkering annually left the Twins with the lowest salary level in baseball, but the Twins were often in the middle of the league standings at season's end. Two points of view emerged amongst baseball watchers:

The Calvin Griffith Upside View: he had the best return on investment (wins per dollar) of any owner in baseball.

The Calvin Griffith Downside View: while other owners were playing to win baseball championships, Calvin Griffith was engaged in a game of pitching pennies and was pleased to go home with a losing record and a five buck profit. (This was, of course, the view of Twins fans).

When it comes to reengineering your business processes, you will have to make a decision that hinges on just this point: are you looking for incremental improvements that will strengthen your existing processes or will you seek something more radical by looking at your business with new eyes?

In order to refine the vision, you should consider the major business processes of your firm and imagine how they might be radically improved. An example of a major process is order fulfillment. Order entry, as a subset of order fulfillment, is usually a minor process. Most firms can break down the spectrum of their activity into less than a dozen major processes and these can be analyzed both separately and collectively. In some cases, one new process may replace multiple existing processes.

Remember that your destination is workflow. If you need refreshing on this, return to the latter pages of the chapter *What*

Is SAP? The greatest enemy of workflow is the attitude of 'this is how we do it here'. If how you do it there is so hot and your futures are all assured, you don't need SAP. Burn this book.

One phase that you should spend little time worrying about is the classic AS-IS (aka How We Work Today). There are implementation methods that stress lengthy AS-IS phases, during which your current processes are charted and scripted to infinite detail. The point is that once you have a complete inventory of all you are, you will see clearly what has to be improved. This is bullroar, and costly bullroar if you assign a full-blown AS-IS to a consulting firm. All you truly need is some charting and scripting of current major processes and maybe some of the more complex sub-processes. This exercise will help the external consultants understand your business and the internal consultants learn charting and scripting. Then you can all wash your hands of the chore and get on with the refining of the vision.

Phase 2: Configuring to Prototype

This is where your BPR rubber hits the SAP road, as your team seeks to configure R/3 to meet the new business process designs. There are more than a thousand potential tables to be set and their interaction is not negligible, so it is very much a Rubik's cube. Therefore, your team will be engaged in an iterative trial-and-error process in which you will find yourselves moving between design and configuration across all modules until you are satisfied. However, project team satisfaction is not the goal; the other business people have to be satisfied as well, and the only way for them to judge with understanding is if they can see the system work. For this and other reasons you will configure to a prototype.

Your prototype will be the visible, tangible proof of concept. It will be used to demonstrate applications, integration, and workflow and will provide a basis for end user education. Entire business processes can be 'rehearsed' and refined. In the long term, the prototype will be used as a "what if" tool to simulate organizational changes and to test them for potential benefit.

The reengineering-configuration loop is the point at which many implementations have bogged down. As the project team seeks to match R/3 to target business practices, the trial-and-error configuring can go on too long. In addition, team members learn more about the vast possibilities of R/3 and can be tempted to add unplanned functionality. This temptation leads to expansion of scope (nothing as slow as scope creep) which also can bog down your progress.

It is at this juncture that a viable gap analysis can be accomplished. You will find that despite the vastness of R/3, it may not address all of the processes in the way you need it to. For each of the identified gaps, your options are:

Option	Advantage	Disadvantage
Acquire additional software	Sounds keen	Interfacing and lack of integration
Modify R/3 with ABAP/4 patches	You get just what you want	You face support and maintenance problems
Accept the gap and customize as best you can	Retain integration; no interfacing or maintenance; await R/3 upgrade	Living with the gap; for how long?

There are difficult decisions to be made and the scope of your project may be altered.

Another school of thought is that this point is too late in the project to complete the gap analysis. From here to the end of the project there may not be time enough to fill the gaps, thus compromising the deadline as well as team harmony. We have no quarrel with this school of thought except that experience has taught us that it is truly during the BPR-configuration exercise that real gaps are identified. Users tend to cling to traditional ways of doing business and will negatively compare theoretic

R/3 to their current operations. When a gap analysis takes place prior to prototyping, all kinds of misperceived gaps are identified, and more time and money are wasted than if a firm waits until this point.

A reengineering-configuring loop. Expansion of scope. A gap analysis. This is where the project manager will make the great difference between failure or success. There are compromises to be made and decisions that will not be universally applauded. Weak management at this point will imperil the overall project. But remember that after core implementation you will still be able to configure and re-configure R/3, so those elements that fall by the wayside now may be recovered at a later time.

One way of avoiding the reengineering-configuring loop is to take advantage of the vast pool of business process templates afforded by SAP. These 'templates' consist of pre-configured elements of R/3 that will satisfy chosen business processes and scenarios. It is often said that these templates are based on 'best business practices'. Whether you agree with this qualification or not, you will find that for most of the business processes you are seeking to configure, a template probably is available, an R/3 Rubik's cube that has already been set to the color scheme you want.

One last note on the subjects of scope and focus:

Normally, you will want to address project scope that will lead to immediate, dramatic benefits, but with limited resources, you may find yourself getting blocked in areas where project ownership is fuzzy. Says David Chapman, "It is a fact that some of your project impetus will depend upon who from your organization jumps into the project and who does not."

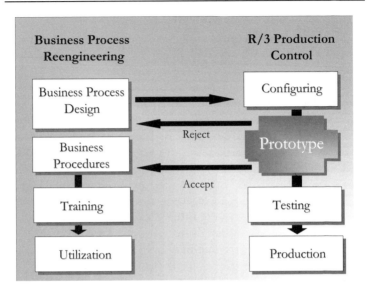

Plan Your Testing

Nancy Bancroft urges people "to include plans for testing and support systems early in the process. I know we have enough trouble trying to get them to think about training early on, but it is important to plan for testing and support as well. I know of one company that planned a month for testing, but the inevitable happened and they found themselves with only a week before the planned go live for data testing. So they tested for a week and went live with a long list of problems. Of course they immediately started to work on the fixes, but other problems cropped up as the users tried to process their transactions. This company is considering suing their implementation partner."

The company mentioned here is also guilty of planning to deadline rather than planning to completion. The dual point is that a) testing is not a last minute final check; it is a major component of success and b) if the system test fails, you should not go live, no matter what deadline is pinned to the wall.

Phase 3: Technical Development

Areas to be addressed through programming and Basis work include:

- ⌐ Interfacing
- ⌐ Migration - Data Conversion
- ⌐ Operational Environment
- ⌐ Customizing
- ⌐ Reporting

If you are retaining certain legacy systems, even for a limited time, you will still need to write **interfaces** between these systems and R/3. Because of the high degree of integration between R/3 applications, this interfacing can be complex and costly.

For legacy systems that are being replaced by R/3, you will have to prepare programs to **convert necessary data**. This can be nightmarish at the level of the materials management master file, for example, because much of the data you will need to take advantage of R/3 probably does not exist. Completing a data manifest is a time-consuming administrative chore, not a technical task, but it bears mentioning here because of the sheer volume of so many materials master records. A typical firm will have between 500 and 2,000 client master records, between 200 and 1,000 supplier master records, anywhere from 50 to 2,000 product records, and anywhere from 1,000 to 200,000 material master records.

As configuration is coming to an end, your hardware platform will be prepared and the **operational environment** put into place at the level of Basis. The 'tuning' of your installation will continue as modules are ready and system use commences. If you are in a large firm and will have several inter-operational sites, you should note that Basis becomes a major issue as the sites multiply. Even experienced Basis administrators have struggled in recent years with many-site R/3 operations. Less experienced Basis administrators have been overwhelmed. The many-site installation is new territory in the world of SAP. R/2 is mainframe-based, but R/3's client/server architecture is not. Balancing and tuning many-site installations will almost certainly require assistance from solid Basis consultants and possibly SAP itself.

Following a gap analysis, you may choose to **customize R/3** with specific ABAP/4 programming. Do so with caution. The software includes certain areas known as "user exits" which are areas that can be customized without endangering your SAP support. Changes to the software outside of these areas may result in your need to perform new maintenance each time you upgrade to a new version of R/3. User exits are taken into account for upgrades. The other areas are not.

Despite the fact that hundreds of standard **reports** are included in the package, and despite the fact that tools such as Query and SAPScript allow for the easy creation of further reports, most firms feel compelled to undertake a certain amount of ABAP/4 programming to allow for 'special customized personalized I cannot live without this listing' reports. I am convinced that there is something seriously askew in the world of business when it comes to reports, i.e. formatted information. In a coming chapter, we detail various levels of SAP education for your firm. One course is not included because no such course yet exists, namely "Information: What It Is, How to Grasp It, and How to Apply It to Business." Few business executives readily admit to needing such a course. No market for it whatsoever.

The Conversion Stage

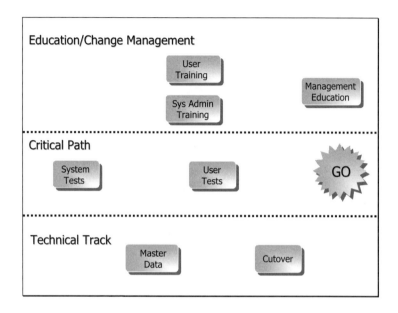

Testing and training are the primary activities of the conversion stage and both of these activities should occur at multiple levels. Timing becomes a major issue for each of these because much of the training depends upon the testing and successful use of the new software, which requires that day one utilization occur shortly after the completion of training.

System Testing

There are three levels of system testing that must take place.

⌐ Module Testing
⌐ Integration Testing
⌐ Stress Testing.

Module testing actually occurs repeatedly during the configuration process, but a formal and final test of each configured module will still reveal wrinkles that need ironing.

Complete business processes are tested in **integration testing**, which reveals discrepancies between modules. Similar to the BPR-configuring loop, you may find yourselves caught in a testing-reconfiguring loop.

Stress testing involves loading the system with more data and more transactions than you will be using. If system performance degrades, Basis help may be required or you may have to tinker with the configuration. Another level of stress testing is to throw wild business scenarios into play (several conflicting sales order modifications, a confusing pattern of delivery requests, etc.) to see whether or not the system breaks down.

Management Preparation

You should envision an effort to prepare management for the imminent conversion to the new system. This does not have to be the object of a formal course or seminar, but you should communicate how the rhythm of work is about to change and continue to stress the importance of continual business improvement, i.e. that even after day one use of R/3, the evolution will continue and probably accelerate.

End User Training and Acceptance

How end user training should occur is covered in Chapter 5: Learning to Swim in the SAP Waters.

The timing of end user training is almost as important as the quality of the training delivered. Wonderfully executed courses will keen the enthusiasm of the users, but that enthusiasm will wane and the lessons will be forgotten if there is too lengthy a lull between the training sessions and actual system use.

The finest SAP trainer I know, Patti Walsh, tells people that as far as she is concerned, SAP means Sit and Play. She always makes time to allow her students to 'sandbox' , which is like test driving a new car. The more time a user can spend playing with the system, the better. Therefore, try to make the system available to end users outside of the training periods in the hope that they will play with it and, in doing so, become more comfortable with navigation and exploitation.

Once end user training is complete, a last form of testing may occur and that is **user acceptance testing**. To this point, all of the testing will have been done by the system builders, but as users settle themselves into their cockpits, elements that system builders (who are not users) did not consider will come to light.

Years ago, a programmer continually delivered faulty programs to a user group I represented. Upon her fourth delivery of an invoice posting program, I bent to the keyboard to test it and simply slapped my palm onto several keys at once. The program bombed. "Users won't do that!" argued the programmer. "I am a user," I replied, "and I just did."

Go Live

Use it, friend, and prosper.

Post-Implementation: the Windfall

It is always a great pleasure to talk to people who have not only succeeded in implementing R/3 but who also continued to help their firms evolve by *using* R/3. All of these people admit that they expected to set down their implementation tools once the core implementation was finished, and were surprised to find that there is a continued acceleration of business improvement AFTER the core implementation. In all cases, these people express how gratifying it is to continuously implement in the course of daily business.

Once the core implementation is complete, it is as though you have just nudged your canoe onto a far shore and the destination of workflow is at last in sight.

Assuming that you have mastered the principle of continuous business improvement, you will find yourselves immersed in ever more beneficial activities. With a working core of R/3, much of the time pressure should be removed and you will be in a position to go back to gaps that could not be addressed in the first go. Further, through your use of R/3, you will identify champions of the software, people who grasp how to take advantage of its features to bring benefit to the firm.

You will also be in a position to consider additional applications that were not included in the core implementation. Applications such as Project System, Quality Maintenance, Plant Maintenance, and Workflow usually fall under this heading.

One post-implementation legacy is the existence of people whose jobs include the management of business processes and the consequent disappearance of 'vertical' management (for discrete business units). Process managers, armed with a functioning R/3, will continue to tinker with the configuration according to opportunity as well as changing business conditions. If you are in top management, you should not view this re-configuring as a pointless perpetuation of the implementation but see it as the sweetest fruit of the endeavor.

Another post-implementation legacy is that people from heretofore disparate sectors will find themselves working together on a daily basis. Representatives from finance, logistics, production planning, transport, et al, who were thrown together for the implementation, will find that their bond is complete and that ongoing, evolutionary configuration of R/3 is a part of their new job descriptions.

Connectivity (ALE-EDI, Internet, or other) usually becomes an opportunity issue after core implementation. Bringing your systems to customers via the Internet can be the most dramatic step of all. As Internet use expands by over 200,000 users per month in North America. Nearly every viable company already has a web site. On-line shopping is expanding exponentially and is taking a market share in the same way that cable television began to take market share from the big three networks in the 1970's.

According to a posting by WebPromote, a division of Superhighway Consulting, Inc., "There are some 47.7 million people on the face of our planet who do not access the Internet in English." What might happen if you:

1. advertise your firm with a solid web page;

2. implement SAP R/3 (with its global functionality, including multi-language screens);

3. allow access to product information and direct ordering via the Internet?

Some companies lumber toward workflow and connectivity, others jog; few sprint. All the same, one of the most exciting times in your firm will probably take place in the first year after core implementation.

One Size Fits All (With Reservations)

Some years ago, SAP launched what was known as the Heidelberg Project, aka SAP Lite. The goal was to develop a streamlined, simpler version of R/3 that could be marketed to small and middle-sized firms. The project was later dropped when SAP recognized that it was founded on the faulty premise that small companies are simpler to manage than large companies and thus need less functionality. In fact, it is the opposite that is true. Smaller firms require broader business skills and more flexibility from their employees than do large firms and business functions are more often crossed and hybridized.

What SAP was seeking to accomplish with the Heidelberg Project was partly in reaction to the North American notion that R/3 is a Big Boy Toy. This notion was underscored by the number of Fortune 500 firms

Company Size	% of SAP
> $2.5B	18%
$1B - $2.5K	17%
$500M- $1B	11%
$200M - $500M	18%
< $200M	36%

Source: SAP

which had snapped up R/3 and whose endeavors were hogging the news space. As mentioned in an earlier chapter, the breakdown of SAP licenses by company size refutes the notion of R/3 as intended only for big companies.

As the chart illustrates, small and mid-sized companies represent 65% of the R/3 licenses and SAP, having rightfully scrapped the Heidelberg Project, is instead concentrating on providing new support for this market group.

Certified Business Solutions

Recognizing the importance of the middle-sized market, SAP America created the Certified Business Solutions program in 1997. The target market for this program encompasses companies between $50 and $200 million revenue in Australia, Canada, and the United States. Such a market is out of the geographic and strategic range of most Big 6 firms but is squarely in the range of the small and midsize SAP consulting firms. With SAP as the parent partner, roughly a dozen of these firms have been made CBS partners, each with a geographic region, and all are working together to penetrate the new market and provide quality implementation assistance and ongoing support.

The challenge for the CBS partners is to successfully implement enterprise-wide software and provide a transfer of SAP knowledge to firms that traditionally have limited IS staff and whose operations do not fit the corporate mold. Yet another challenge is to implement swiftly because these mid-sized firms cannot absorb consulting and education costs in the way that large firms do.

Other cost and implementation factors that come into play for small and middle-size firms:

⌐ Smaller companies are more flexible and susceptible to successful business process reengineering than are large firms. This factor alone can go a long way toward reducing consulting costs.

⌐ Smaller companies cannot pay huge license fees, but SAP addresses this with its pricing structure, which is largely based upon the number of users.

⌐ Smaller companies cannot pay high consulting fees for a lengthy duration and *must* assure a rapid transfer of SAP knowledge from their consultants.

⌐ Smaller companies are seldom in a position to provide in-house staff full time to SAP implementation projects, which hampers the transfer of SAP knowledge.

⌐ Smaller companies do not use the same large platforms that have been at the core of the large firm installations. However, SAP's strength in cross-platform technology, its 1995 release of an AS/400 version, and its fit with UNIX will put it in good stead.

SAP sold 200 such licenses in 1997 and projects another 345 for 1998.

If the CBS program continues to succeed, and there is every reason to believe that it will, there is one predictable speed bump of major height that will be encountered: another serious shortage of qualified SAP consultants to satisfy the demand. This will not only be felt in terms of the numbers of consultants, but also in their geographic distribution. Further, the experience of most SAP consultants has been in the larger firms, where module specialization is sufficient. New dance steps will be required if these consultants are to succeed in smaller firms, where broader business sense and more adaptable team concepts are required.

How Rapid SAP R/3 Implementation Methods Can Be Misleading

In the spring of 1997, SAP America unveiled its new methodology for implementing R/3. It is called Accelerated SAP or ASAP for short. Thus, SAP

> I once put instant coffee in a microwave and almost went back in time.
> Steven Wright.

itself leapt into the fray of 'rapid' R/3 implementation methods, like so many of its own consulting partners.

In 1995, the drums of the North American press began to pound out an impatient rhythm: SAP takes an eternity to implement. In 1996, that pounding turned to a steady, *noisy* beat and here we are nowadays with rapidfastspeedyinstant methods to a) envision a new enterprise, b) re-engineer according to that vision, c) educate and re-deploy the employee populace to new business processes, d) configure R/3 on an enterprise-wide scale e) migrate from legacy systems and f) whew, seize the benefits.

Would you like fries with that?

The truth is, no such implementation can succeed in less than one year, no matter how small the enterprise, no matter how many armies of consultants are thrown into the trenches, no matter how committed your management may be. This is not a question of methods or expertise, but of human nature.

An R/3 implementation engenders major changes in the way an enterprise functions. These changes are bewildering to many, unwanted by some, and difficult to adapt even by those who are fully on board. Change management, often derided as an eighties frivolity, takes center stage in successful SAP implementations. Career paths are altered, new business skills must be learned, resistance must be flattened without brutality, and new business processes must be understood and put into play. Someone call up Alvin Toffler. Future shock, when it comes to SAP, is very real.

Too often, clients asks consultants how long it will take to put "it" "in", a spurious question from any angle. If "it" is SAP R/3, what configuration will take place and according to what business processes? Is "it" a complete suite of core applications (i.e. financials and logistics) or will "it" also include Project System, Plant Maintenance, Workflow, an Executive Information System, Internet access capacity, and a score of modifications that the HR director insists upon. Will "it" be defined once, during project master planning, or will "it" be redefined throughout the project according to changes in scope brought on by changes in the business climate?

> SAP R/3 can be stuffed into your enterprise like a forty inch beer waist into thirty inch designer jeans (with the same discomfiting results).

In the real world, "it" tends to be an amorphous blob that no three people could describe in a similar fashion.

Now, what about the definition of "in"?

If "in" is defined as functioning, with what benefit to your enterprise? Does "in" mean that data has been transferred from old systems to new? Is "in" the first day anyone uses a single application, or have you achieved "in" only after all planned applications are running? Have you reached a state of "in" when the first report unfurls on a laser printer or does "in-ness" descend upon your firm when the first economic benefits are realized? Do process failures hedge "in" bets?

Of course, SAP R/3 can be stuffed into your enterprise like a forty inch beer waist into thirty inch designer jeans (with the same discomfiting results). Simply adopt the business practices addressed by your out-of-the-box R/3 configuration and bend your staff like beasts to that vision and "it" is "in". Such a stuffing can take as little as three months. Just don't let your breath out.

The length of time it takes to truly implement SAP R/3 will be determined by a combination of a great many factors, most of them having to do with how well your team (from management to the implementation team) works in cohesion. Is the goal visible and tangible and measurable, or is it soft and chewy (as in "to become a world class outfit")? Are the consultants engaged in transferring SAP knowledge to client staff or perpetuating their presence on site? Has the BPR-configuring team been given sufficient education or merely a few classes at SAP America? Is there a distinction between a critical mass implementation and the subsequent continuing process improvement cycle, or are you clinging to the notion that once "it" is "in", you can pack up the toolbox and head off to the café?

Accelerated SAP (ASAP) promises its followers a six-month implementation cycle. With ASAP, the "it" that goes "in" is the establishment of core SAP functions (finance and logistics) but not necessarily the reengineering of processes to take advantage of workflow. To its credit, the method foregoes the AS-IS phase and there is a treasure trove of tools that *will* help you to speed up the process, such as a pre-canned project plan, an exhaustive inventory of business processes (related to R/3 module chains), and a large number of template forms and procedures. Further, ASAP is built as a Microsoft Office™ kit, including Word documents, Excel spreadsheets, MS Project plans, and PowerPoint slide shows. It is possible to tweak the method by either including other documents or revising those that are offered to suit your needs and context..

Once this methodology was released, consulting firms immediately raced to complete implementations faster and faster and the marketing world was dotted with ads and announcements like "Roadrunner Corporation Completes SAP Implementation

During Long Lunch Break!". Note that rapidity, speed, *acceleration* are the keys to this methodology. The five basic steps are:

1. Project Preparation
2. Business Blueprint
3. Realization
4. Final Preparation
5. Go Live

The point to this method is that SAP can be fitted to your company in practically an AS-IS state. The TO BE, including business process reengineering, will come later, if at all.

"In essence," says Betty Costa, "the ASAP methodology plans for the organization to readily adapt to the SAP process without any formal business process reengineering."

The upside to following this method is that you will avoid many of the pitfalls engendered by a lengthy implementation. The downside is that you will not seize the full and serious benefits offered by a truer implementation.

Admittedly, there is no hard and fast rule as to when reengineering should occur, before, during, or after core implementation of R/3. Still, if the dramatic benefits of R/3 are what you have in mind, then business process reengineering should take place at some point in time. Witness...

From an interview of Nancy Bancroft (author of *Implementing SAP R/3*) with Jon Reed of Allen Davis & Associates:

Reed: Do you think it's possible to do a technical implementation of SAP without addressing the reengineering issues?

Bancroft: Some companies have insisted that yes, they have simply implemented exactly the way that they were running their business, that the changes they had to make were incidental. But you will change your business- you will! Everybody will make certain changes in their business processes as a result of SAP. I don't know of anybody that hasn't, but some people say 'we have done a vanilla kind of implementation and if we need any reengineering we'll do it later.'

I've got a lot of suspicion about that, a lot of doubts about the wisdom of approaching it that way. But suppose you're under the gun, you have to have the thing up by the end of the year because you're bringing a new product line on. So if you're under the gun, then it falls in the category of 'there isn't any choice, we just have to get this thing up and if we have to make changes in our business, we'll just have to make them later.' There are legitimate reasons for taking that posture. But the concern I have is that the amount of going back, backing up, backtracking, basically re-configuring the system because you've decided to make significant changes in the way you do business- there's a cost, there's a cost to doing that.

(reprinted with the permission of Jon Reed and Nancy Bancroft)

Client expectations are not easy to manage or to meet. Rapid or accelerated implementations will necessarily exclude the more difficult aspects of a standard implementation and lay a greater burden on client and consulting staff, though for a briefer time period. If you are pondering the implementation of SAP software as the support to a reengineered enterprise, you may still use the Accelerated SAP method, but you do not have to adhere entirely to its timetable or content.

Accelerated implementation methods are not the question here. Indeed, it is great to see that consulting firms are learning to cut to the chase with new approaches to 'making it work'. Beginning in the summer of 1997 and in accelerating numbers during the fall, successful ASAP-guided implementations occurred throughout North America and client satisfaction has risen sharply. However, client expectations have to be tempered at the same time and we therefore underscore the point that the ultimate "it" is the re-invention of an enterprise and an SAP implementation, though crucial, is only a subset of that "it".

Project elements that will accelerate an implementation:

1	Visible, measurable criteria for success
2	Mastery of scope
3	Transfer of SAP knowledge from consultant to client
4	ASAP - for its accelerator tools.

Chapter 4

The Wild West of SAP Consulting

- ⏌ A Brief History of SAP Consulting in North America
- ⏌ What SAP Consultants Do
- ⏌ When SAP is $AP
- ⏌ Choosing Your SAP Consultants Wisely
- ⏌ Trends in SAP Consulting
- ⏌ Post-Adolescence for SAP Consulting

The Wild West of SAP Consulting

"I don't fly on Thursdays."
-an SAP Consultant to her boss.

A Brief History of SAP Consulting in North America

SAP's previous offering, R/2, was a mainframe-based product that was very successful in Europe, Australia, and South Africa, but not all that successful in North America. Thus, when R/3 was announced in late 1992, there was only a small base of R/2 consultants on the entire continent. Since that time, the well-known shortage of SAP consultants has persisted as SAP licensing has continued unabated.

In the world of consulting, SAP has been $AP, but the rush of many to join in the monetary fun has given a black eye to much of the practice, not only because of the high consulting rates but because of spotty performances by a number of the firms.

In the "early" years of 1993 and 1994, the myth was still in place that R/3 was just another hot software package. Therefore, IS staff was being converted to SAP. It was not until 1995 that it became more generally understood that success with R/3 requires business sense, not technical know-how. Still, the majority of firms are looking at IS background as a necessity.

The early players were the Big 6 firms, primarily Price Waterhouse, ICS Deloitte, Andersen Consulting, and, to a lesser degree, Ernst & Young and KPMG (in addition to Andersen Consulting and IBM). Their global alliances with SAP AG and the initial flood of Fortune 500 firms to SAP dictated the need for large consulting firms. SAP opened partner academies in Dallas and Boston, offering a six-week program that churned out 'certified' consultants by the hundreds, but as countless Fortune 500 clients can attest, 'certified' did not always equate to 'qualified.'

By 1995, smaller SAP-dedicated firms began to spring up in greater and greater numbers: Clarkston Potomac, Kelly-Levey Associates, SCP, HJM, and dozens of others. But as the need for experienced SAP consultants was all the more evident, European firms took up residence in North America and provided a major boost to the market. Prominent among these were Origin and Bureau Van Dijk. Other North American firms recruited consultants from previous R2 hotbeds such as Europe, Australia, and South America. Results from foreign consultants have been mixed. Many of the European consultants are certainly SAP-savvy but are not particularly sensitive to the consulting requirements in North America.

As of the end of 1997, there are over two hundred SAP consulting "practices" in North America, of which less than sixty are true professional practices. The remainder are body shop organizations or companies that list SAP consulting as part of their repertoire but which do not have any viable presence on the market. Within the next three years, it is probable that only about one hundred of these companies will still be standing. As the demand curve flattens and clients become more demanding and discerning, SAP consulting practices will have to become more professional and adhere to the same standards as other consulting practices.

Thus, short term gains have been made by firms without a complete professional practice; long-term survival will depend upon the establishment of standards and practices that have not been developed until recently.

What SAP Consultants Do

In an ideal world, SAP consultants provide a transfer of their SAP knowledge to the client until that client is self-sufficient, and then they disappear.

At the opposite end of the spectrum, SAP consultants turn your company into a laboratory environment in which they impose their methods and madness, leaving chaos and human debris in their wake, and then they send along a mammoth invoice.

Between these two poles, there is a lot to work with but let's concentrate on the ideal in hopes of avoiding its opposite.

There are essentially three time-frames in which SAP consultants can be crucial to your success in implementing R/3:

During the *planning stage*, senior consultants provide guidance for budgeting, team formation, the establishment of realistic expectations, and the creation of a do-able project master plan. They establish a foundation of coherent terminology and help you to express the vision of the endeavor to the company body.

During the *business development stage*, module consultants provide a transfer of SAP knowledge to client staff and shorten the learning curve in regard to business process reengineering and the subsequent configuring of R/3 to reflect that reengineering.

During the *technical development stage*, Basis, network, and ABAP/4 consultants provide services that support the frame of the business development. Many companies outsource such services, even after completion of core implementation.

Education embraces all three of these time-frames and is at the heart of correct employ of consultants. This subject will be covered in Chapter 5: Learning to Swim in the SAP Waters.

If properly utilized, few consultants are still around when you throw the post-implementation party. Having provided a boost to your staff, an acceleration of events, and a meaningful transfer of SAP knowledge, they should have long since said their goodbyes.

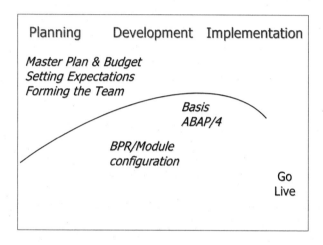

The accent must be on transfer of knowledge so that you can reduce your dependency upon consultants. For example, module configuration should be *guided* by consultants, not handed over to them lock, stock, and barrel; if so, you will not be in a position to modify configurations once the consultants are gone. Time and budget pressures often lead client staff to accelerate events by unleashing the consultants (leaving it to the experts) but the short-term gains will be paid for in the long term.

When SAP is $AP

The exploding SAP market and the consequent massive shortfall of experienced R/3 consultants have given rise to an unhealthy subculture, driven largely by greed, which makes it difficult for clients to sort through their consulting options.

These are some of the highjinks you run into on a weekly basis when swimming the often murky SAP consulting waters:

Bait and switch: A firm bidding to become a client's implementation partner promotes star consultants during the proposal phase and sends inferior consultants once the deal is set.

Flooding the zone: A firm assigns one or two star consultants to a project and surrounds them with an army of neophyte consultants whose SAP experience can be measured in weeks. It takes a while for the client to recognize this because at the onset of a project, neophytes *seem* to know so much more than the client, but mostly they are hiding behind a terminology smoke-screen.

Gin rummy (spades) : A haves-and-needs body shopper sends a subcontract consultant to a client; some time later, the body shopper finds a cheaper consultant for the same job and, through some pretext, replaces the first one for greater personal profit.

Gin rummy (clubs): A contract consultant accepts a six-month assignment. Two months into the job, the consultant finds another assignment that pays more. Citing 'philosophical differences', he/she abandons the first client in mid-project.

Casper Consulting, Inc.: Resumes of non-existant consultants are presented to clients to puff up the size of a consulting roster. Not so curiously, these consultants are always 'on another assignment'.

Sap, not SAP: Resumes are sprinkled with SAP initials like SD, MM, or PP but the candidate has no real SAP experience. This gambit is widespread since anyone who can fake their way into a job will get the requisite experience toward making the resume true. A candidate once called me and opened his spiel by saying that he had three years of *sap* experience. That's what he said, sap (rhymes with zap), not SAP. He means to put the moves on me and he cannot even pronounce it correctly? Imagine the resonance of a phone slamming onto its receiver.

Facing Mirrors(((()))): There are great numbers of contract consultants who cut subcontract representation deals with more than one consulting firm and thus appear on several firms' rosters. These consultants are only slightly more available than those from Casper Consulting, Inc.

Recruiting consultants for SAP consulting firms is also an adventure in the skin trade. The demands of candidates are often laughable and just as often out of this world. One prospective recruit asked that a certified check for $2,000 be presented to him upon his arrival at the airport *for an interview*. The consultant who would not fly on Thursdays later refused any assignment outside of Manhattan. Another consultant specified the minimum acceptable square footage of his hotel rooms, the minimum acceptable range of rental car, and the maximum acceptable travel miles in any given month. His requisite bonus schedule was, of course, a sight to see.

Rob Doane, the resource manager for the Holland Technology Group, relates the story of a consultant with two years of SAP who asked for $250 per hour. Rob's response: "Are you twins?"

(Yet another consultant -at the strange edge of another spectrum altogether- insisted upon staying in a youth hostel rather than the hotel assigned by the client, stating that a good hotel was a wasteful expense.)

There is a West Coast SAP haves-and-needs bodyshopper that I often refer to as The Man Who Never Stops Laughing. In 1995, he was an executive search specialist, but he finally switched over to the placement of SAP contract consultants. His overhead consists of an office, a computer, a web-site, and some very high phone bills. Whenever I call him, he giggles some about his good fortune and, because I am a writer and he thinks of me as an SAP prognosticator, he asks me "How long will this SAP thing last?"

The "SAP thing" he is referring to is the low supply and high demand for consultants. Two years ago, I assured him that he had at least three more years. Recently, I told him he had at least three more years. (So much for *that* SAP prognostication.)

Contract consultants usually want $100 to $150 an hour and this gentleman's take for finding them clients is about $15 for each hour that they bill. With anywhere from twenty to thirty people working for him at a time, his income is around $400 an hour. Now you know why he never stops laughing.

Choosing Your SAP Consultants Wisely

Flip through any stack of candidate resumes and you will almost surely find at least one that fits the categories we have described. Gleaning the SAP wheat from the $AP chaff is not as hard as it may seem.

Your first question is whether or not you will form a team from the vast pool of contract consultants or retain the services of an SAP consulting firm. Most clients, skittish about consulting to begin with, choose the latter because they want a single accountable source.

Selection criteria for an SAP consulting firm are:

⌐ Size
⌐ SAP Experience
⌐ Consulting Experience
⌐ Project Method
⌐ Industry Background

You will gain little insight about any of these from brochures or websites and not much more from PowerPoint presentations offered by prospective firms, so a little digging is required.

1. Size

Does the firm have sufficient resource to staff your project from beginning to end?

For the Fortune 500 set, the answer to this question has been and remains 'No'. All Fortune 500 SAP implementations have been multi-partner endeavors with one company filling the role of 'lead partner'.

Even for small and mid-sized firms, the shortage of available consultants is such that most teams have to be augmented by contract or subcontract staff.

What you want to avoid is the company that gathers a crew from Zanzibar, Hong Kong, and the Gold Coast and pretends that the 'team' they are proposing is their standard product.

One of the troubles with Fortune 500 firms is that management level people often think of themselves as "Fortune 500" managers; consulting interlopers from (necessarily) smaller firms are often entertained with stories of the big problems faced by big managers in such big firms with such big stakes. The scale that slides to make the frog fit the pond. I am convinced that if Jesus Christ and the twelve disciples returned today in the form of a change management consulting firm with a service that guaranteed the client that its employees would work in perfect, profit-making, harmony, some doofus in a Fortune 500 firm would turn them down because their outfit was "too small".

2. SAP Experience

This is slippery territory because the value behind experience is difficult to gauge. When someone has twenty years of experience, is it varied and evolutionary experience, or is it one year of experience repeated twenty times?

It is recommended that you interview each prospective consultant before accepting him or her on the project. If you do not have enough knowledge of SAP to conduct such an interview, hire a third party consultant to do it for you. Further, ask for references and follow up on them. There is no better way for you to confirm a consultant's background.

3. Consulting Experience

SAP battlefields are littered with consultants who originally gained their skills while implementing in their own company and then converted to consulting. Many of these are excellent resources, but not all of them have sufficient consulting skills to be truly effective. It is one thing to implement R/3 in a firm that you know inside and out and another thing to parachute into a company, learn about it from the ground up, and provide semi-instants results.

In short, industry experience with SAP does not automatically qualify someone as a viable SAP consultant.

This Diamond Ring...

SAP has an alliance partnership program in which there are logo partners, global partners, national partners, and CBS partners. Until mid-1997, this program made little sense in that the rules for partnership were poorly defined and badly applied. Some SAP consulting firms with more than 50 consultants were denied partnership, while one of the national partners had only one SAP consultant. Now, obtaining partnership status is simplified, but annual reviews of performance determine whether or not partnership will be retained. Further, SAP is pushing for partner firms to have their consultants 'ASAP Certified', which requires a course in ASAP method. All the same, it is not essential that the consulting firm you choose have the 'SAP Partner' label. What is more important is the level of SAP experience and sound business knowledge that the assigned consultants can offer.

4. Project Method

Assess the method or approach that the prospective firm is offering. Is it Accelerated SAP? Is it a method that is "Powered by ASAP"? The latter is a tag that means "we took some of the philosophy of ASAP and plugged it into our existing method". Is it a paper-driven method or are PC tools incorporated? Is the method flexible enough to address your concerns? Does it underscore transfer of SAP knowledge or does it call for consultants to do it all from A to Z?

If the prospective firm asks you to pay for use of its methodology, eliminate it from consideration. Likewise if the method offered includes a lengthy AS-IS phase.

6. Industry Background

More and more, R/3 is becoming industry-specific and the configuration varies from industry to industry. Oil & gas, automotive, retail, process manufacturing, health care, utilities, etc. Many consultants can perform across a wide spectrum, but it will be of obvious benefit if your consulting team already has experience in your industry. We recommend that you not push the industry envelope too far. A client once informed to me that he needed consultants with experience in metals mining (fair enough) but also insisted that they have background in nickel and tungsten alloy manufacture and that they relocate to New Mexico.

Trends in North American SAP Consulting

1. Y2K

An unquantified (but clearly visible) driver for SAP sales has been the Year 2K debacle. Many firms which might have hesitated to choose SAP have found that it is preferable to implement SAP at great cost than to correct Y2K problems at similar cost.

2. Market Shift

The Fortune 500 SAP market is becoming saturated, and the CBS program (targeting small to mid-sized firms) is just underway. It is probable that new implementations for the larger firms will begin to tail off by 1999, but the small and middle-sized markets are already opening up and this business will fill the void.

One major element in this market shift is the need for SAP consultants with broader business background than those who have populated the large firm implementations. Limited specialization will prove too costly for smaller implementations because smaller firms cannot pay for large implementation teams and would not tolerate narrow specialization anyway.

3. Continuous Implementations

Since the beginning of 1997, a number of implementations have moved into phase 2 modules (PS, PM, PP-PI, etc.) and demand for these specialists, as well as for HR, is on a mid-term rise. The completion of North American payroll has led to a flood of demand for HR specialists that should continue for some years to come.

4. Basis

Basis consulting is eternal in that many companies either fail to adequately address their long-term Basis requirements or prefer to outsource. Further, as global implementations are being rolled out, a variety of Basis problems are arising and these problems have outstripped clients' capacity to solve them. It is useless to look for overseas consultants because the R/3 experience (in Basis) is just as new to Europeans as it is to North Americans.

5. ASAP and Other Accelerated Methods

Client impatience and confusion about business process reengineering has given rise to an attitude in which R/3 is implemented with little or no reengineering. Without BPR, the dramatic benefits offered by R/3 are set aside for a later time. It is probable that clients will be a) more satisfied with the consulting effort while b) being less satisfied with SAP unless the two-step approach is firmly established. Consultants who are capable of providing a solid transfer of knowledge will move to the forefront. Consultants who prefer to "do it" for the client will be shunted aside.

6. SAP Education

SAP education could be the fastest growing market over the next few years. SAP America cannot keep up with the demand for quality training and this has been exacerbated by a lack of education sources for management, implementation teams, and direct users.

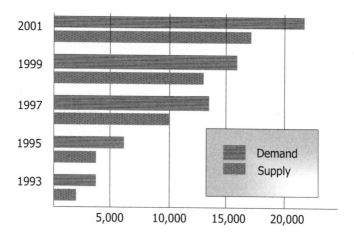

All SAP Consultants - North America

7. Continued Shortfall

SAP's energetic cultivation of the small to mid-sized market will offset a flattening of demand in the Fortune 500 world as well as the drop-off that will occur as Y2K driven projects dry up. Further, a number of major implementations are gearing up, most notably that of General Motors, which has already announced its intention to implement SAP financials globally. The number of consultants needed for such a project will have a direct impact on the remainder of the SAP consulting world. Further, SAP is fast becoming a favored option for government operations. You can expect a rising trend of public sector implementations.

8. Web, Internet, Java...

As firms are moving beyond core implementation, taking advantage of Internet and SAP R/3 is a horizon that is rapidly unscrolling. To some degree, this is all mixed up in the techno-meld of business and communications. To a greater and more direct degree, this is the consulting field that will be tapped by firms with vision beyond the by now clichéd notion of 2000.

Jon Reed's foreseen trends include:

- Post-live investments by Fortune 500 firms in SAP-external 'cutting edge' projects such as Internet commerce, ALE-EDI electronic commerce, and more subsequent applications like sales force automation.

- SAP supply-chain management.

"Basically," he adds, "if SAP plays its cards right, it will succeed in tapping the Fortune 500 for one more round by extending the workflow concept through the back end and cut the front end."

What this may signify is a new and rising shortage of consultants with a diversity of SAP, Internet, and distribution skills and a continuing market in the high end, long range projects.

Post-Adolescence for SAP Consulting

From 1992 to the end of 1996, the failures of SAP consulting were considerable. R/3 was too new and few people knew how it worked, yet waves of inexperienced consultants debarked at Fortune 500 clients and earned their bones in a trial-by-error fashion. Implementation methods for traditional IS acquisition and development projects were applied to R/3 implementations, usually with costly results. The notion of business process reengineering was also new and workflow was barely discussed.

In 1997, we witnessed a maturing at three levels of the SAP world. First, clients began to appreciate the differences between SAP and what they knew before it. Second, SAP America pitched in by hiring and training hundreds of consultants and by forming the Team SAP concept. Finally, the quality of SAP consulting improved through a combination of experience (those people who were rookies in 1993 now possessed four years of SAP experience) and method. The AS-IS phase (a staple of Big 6 firms in which existing procedures are charted and scripted just before being scrapped for the TO-BE vision) fell into general disrepute. The attraction of European consultants is fading as North American R/3 expertise has equaled theirs and none of the consultants I've met in recent months has an aversion to flying on Thursdays.

There will continue to be a market for SAP consultants within the Fortune 500 world. New releases of SAP software, new technology, and the continuing globalization of business will result in subsequent implementation waves even for those firms that think they have finished implementing.

The new horizon, however, is the fertile field of small and mid-sized firms. SAP consultants who have previously found themselves in major cities will become familiar with places like Wichita, New Orleans, Omaha, Sacramento, and Toledo as North American SAP consulting moves into a more mature, and less Wild West, phase.

Next up? The Roaring 20's?

CHAPTER 5

Learning to Swim in the SAP Sea

⌐ Swimming Lessons or Lifeboats

⌐ Executives Are Seldom Taught But They Can Learn

⌐ Education for Middle Management

⌐ Course Customization, Environments and Supports

⌐ Modes of Education

⌐ Project Team Training

⌐ Skills Migration for IS Staff

⌐ End User Training

⌐ The Cost of SAP Education

⌐ The Cost of Lousy Training

Learning to Swim in the SAP Sea

Swimming Lessons or Lifeboats

You were thinking of skipping this chapter or, at best, skimming it. Already your fingers were reaching to page ahead to something more 'compelling'.

Don't do it. The remainder of this book loses its useful luster if SAP education is swept under the rug. Consider this would you invest $100,000 in a Lamborghini and then entrust it to someone without a driver's license? This is just what many firms have done by making a multi-million dollar investment in SAP software and consulting while providing relative crumbs for associated education. Later, when their Lamborghini fails to reach high speed or, worse, crashes into the garage door, it is usually the consultants, those easy targets, who are given the blame.

Moreover, most firms base their training budgets and scenarios on the 'last war' basis, still thinking of the training that was provided for systems that preceded SAP R/3. That is to say, they think only of end user training and neglect the other necessary waves of education that are called for. By the same token, most training is geared to the latter stages of an implementation project, but a more effective schedule calls for layered phases of training/education according to the evolution of the project.

Level	SAP	Change Mgmt	When
Executive	Understand the new enterprise	Develop the vision Share the vision	Acquisition Planning Stage
Middle Mgmt	Continuous reengineering	How to exploit MIS	Planning stage
Supervisors	How to seize benefits-workflow	Supervise change Form new career paths	Development stage
Project team	Module training Integration/team training	Consulting skills	Planning stage
Direct Users	Module training Integration	Business perspective New career path	Implementation stage

Executives Are Seldom Taught But They Can Learn

Since early 1996, I have offered an SAP executive seminar that ranges in length from half a day to two days. The subjects largely cover those that are included in this book but the sessions are tailored to audience size, nature, and need. When this seminar was first conceived, it was assumed that it would be sought by firms that were considering SAP and so felt a need to learn more about it. Surprisingly, the majority of companies that sign up for the seminar are those that have already endeavored to implement SAP and are finding that a major hurdle is the ignorance of their own management. Either the project is being stalled because of management misunderstanding of the venture or the project is succeeding at the implementation level but management is in the dark about what is taking place. Again, senior management tends to acquire SAP and then leaves it to the experts to "put in". The result is seldom pretty.

It is highly recommended that senior management be roped into a useful seminar at the beginning of the project, but if this cannot be arranged, a seminar or course should be made available to these people just as the core implementation is coming to a close. This after-the-fact education will be like offering a surprise to those people who would, ideally, have been supporting you all along. The reality is, they probably will not have much idea what it is the project team has been up to.

The thrust and content of senior management education should be:

⌐ an exposition of the historical and business context of SAP
⌐ a revelation of the critical differences between SAP and traditional systems and the consequent impact on their organizations
⌐ the benefits of workflow as the heart of the matter
⌐ the import and content of change management and a delineation of their role in this context.

It is probable that the greatest impediment to such education will be the unwillingness of senior management to invest the time for it. Senior management usually wants 'nugget' information, summary data, or overviews, and will wrongly assume that 'management education to SAP' is going to consist of a detailed technical presentation concerning *software*. Coaxing senior managers to learn something is a tough task, but it can be made easier if the lead subject of the seminar (don't call it a course, senior managers do not attend 'courses') is something other than 'SAP'. Call it a "Seminar on the New State of Absolutely Everything in this Company" and you might get a positive RSVP.

Education for Middle Management

Middle management is usually comprised of individuals whose patience with an SAP implementation will be the most tested. It is they who are keeping an eye on the budget and timescale and it is on their desks that complaints and conflicts will land. In most instances, it is also this group that has the distinct notion that the implementation will have a visible endpoint and will, in essence, be *over.*

The education required for this group addresses two timeframes of effort: during core implementation and after core implementation.

The content of education for middle management should include much of the same as for senior management, while offering more detail in terms of:

⌙ the intricacies and benefits of workflow

⌙ the concept of continuous reengineering

⌙ implementation blueprints

⌙ case study laboratory.

Supervisors fall under the same category for education, whether or not they participate in the seminars with middle management or are trained separately.

Course Customization, Environments, & Supports

Rather than creating two or three separate courses, you should prepare a master course broken into interrelated sessions. Each level of management course will therefore be a collection of sessions that can be easily configured to meet specific group needs. A course given to commercial executives will necessarily include more commercial (sales, marketing, etc.) context than will a course given to people from manufacturing. Prior to the performance of each course, you should:

⌐ establish the nature of the audience

⌐ establish the intended outcomes of your educational endeavor

⌐ determine which segments should be included in each seminar

⌐ determine the depth of detail required for each segment

⌐ add relevant group context to the entirety of the seminar.

For this last point, we recommend that one or more segments be presented (or co-presented) by staff from the group being taught.

Each course should be a combination of lecture and exercise, using a visual support such as PowerPoint as well as a color handout which includes:

⌐ reproduction of slides and space for notes

⌐ exercise material

⌐ support documents (text) in addendum.

Color handouts work better than black and white for the simple reason that people tend not to throw away color material, whereas black and white is routinely tossed.

A multiple choice and true/false exam at the conclusion of the course is optional, but is usually perceived as an insult by participants.

Modes of Education

Standard course

Lecture and exercise with PowerPoint support and a workbook. Each course would consist of:

❑ SAP Core segment

❑ Your firm's core segment (based upon the Project Charter)

❑ Business sector or division segment.

Audio Tapes

"Rush Hour SAP" - using the same content as the standard course, broken into 30 or 45 minute segments. The attention span for an audio tape is around 20 minutes if the content is standard, so you may want to allow for natural 'breaks'.

Scripts might be based upon the standard course and in addition to a main narrator, the business sector segment would be narrated by relevant management staff.

One obvious impediment to audio tapes is your inability to present visual aids such as charts. Thus, if audio tapes are used, you should consider distributing print handouts as supplements.

Video

Create a video of the standard course, edited to four hours, accompanied by a text support that allows the viewer to follow charts and diagrams.

PowerPoint CBT Course

An at-your-own-speed multi-media slide presentation, with accelerations (branches to various segments).

Books and Documents

Core text (general SAP enlightenment); for example, this book, in conjunction with your firm's core text, the project charter.

Town Hall Meetings

Your executives would receive education via any of the modes previously listed. Consequently, they would be in a position to hold Town Hall Meetings, half hour chats with groups of ten to twelve employees at a time, to present company ambitions vis-à-vis SAP, elaborate upon the plan, and take questions and comments. In addition to providing SAP education to the employee body, Town Hall meetings go a long way toward unraveling the knots of change management.

Project Team Training

Rigorous, multi-level education of your SAP Project Team is an investment that leads to continual returns. If this training is properly completed, your firm will not only be in a position to effectively implement SAP, but also to seize SAP benefits on an ongoing basis.

The benefits of team training, in addition to SAP module training, are numerous:

1. A reduction of configuration time due to a heightened awareness of integration points within SAP and a greater awareness of individual roles and responsibilities.

2. A reduction of customizing or modifications due to improved internal consulting skills

3. The establishment of an accent on benefits and return-on-investment.

4. The formation of a team mentality prior to field work, which reduces trial-and-error.

5. The probable retention of project staff after the core implementation is completed.

The following chart describes the path that we strongly recommend.

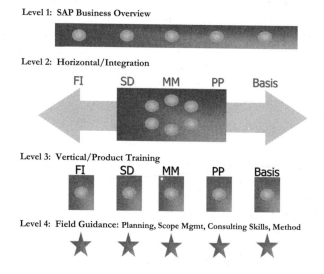

Level 1: SAP Business Overview

Level 2: Horizontal/Integration

FI   SD   MM   PP   Basis

Level 3: Vertical/Product Training

FI   SD   MM   PP   Basis

Level 4: Field Guidance: Planning, Scope Mgmt, Consulting Skills, Method

Phase One: Take it from the Top

The business basics of SAP should be established at the very beginning. The project team should be given the same seminar that is offered to senior and middle management. Module-specific training which follows will be of great use for the daily nuts and bolts of implementation, but unless a distinctly identifiable business environment is established, the subsequent configuration exercise may drift.

The SAP implementation team overview should focus on:

⌟ the intricacies of workflow
⌟ implementation blueprints
⌟ case study laboratory
⌟ the pitfalls of an SAP implementation
⌟ the business process reengineering/configuration iterative loop.

Phase Two: Seeing with a Horizontal View

Configuration skills are not limited to individual modules because of the high degree of integration that is the core of SAP R/3. Thus, prior to SAP level 2 and 3 module training, team members should receive a course in integration and configuration.

Some courses exist that last two weeks and provide an instructor-guided microcosm of an SAP implementation at the level of configuration and integration. Wherever you find such courses, make certain that the principle of business workflow is clearly demonstrated across the horizontal flow of SAP R/3.

An education *experience* such as a learning environment configuration and testing of a system will be the most useful activity at this point. Giving your team members a hands-on experience with the core modules FI, SD, MM, PP will provide far more benefit than would lecture or reading.

Phase 3: The Vertical View

Depending upon assigned roles, various team members will be schooled in specific areas such as FI, SD, MM, or PP. Such training usually includes two levels, the first of which is module overview and the second is module mastery. Configuring SAP's individual modules is at the heart of this training and it should be noted that training alone will not always suffice to prepare an individual for the demands of a project. There is no substitute for configuring experience.

Such training is still in short supply as even SAP America is overwhelmed with demand. Therefore, you may find yourselves even more dependent upon experienced consultants for a transfer of SAP knowledge.

Phase 4: Field Guidance

This last phase of training, which generally lasts about five days, prepares your team in the areas of realistic project and phase planning, scope management, consulting skills, and the application of sound methodology. Without this training, you will have a cadre of SAP-savvy employees who will nevertheless be unprepared for the smell of configuring gunpowder, the rattling of consultant sabers, the trumpet blasts of user meetings, or the lightning fires of scope changes; in short, all that will occur in the project that does not directly address the product.

Consulting skills should not be neglected; without them, your SAP project team member may fail. A case in point: a European SAP consultant I once knew had over five years of experience in FI. At a key point in a project, he found himself unable to convince client staff why certain steps had to be taken for their system to work they way they wanted to. His tactic with the client was to pound the table and tell them that he knew SAP and they did not, so they should take his word as Bible. This is the case of a team member who had sufficient training in levels 1 through 3 but clearly insufficient training for the all-important level 4.

At the conclusion of these four levels of training, you will have a project team that is ready for a final test.

Field Testing the Project Team

Team training for SAP implementation groups is a fairly new concept that is gaining currency because of the success that many firms have had. Team members will have to present themselves as consultants as well as SAP specialists and they will have to work as an integrated team because of the highly-integrated nature of SAP. Without team training, you will have a cluster of module specialists, all knowledgeable in their own subjects but largely ignorant of the fully horizontal picture.

What we recommend is a final consequential training phase in which your team members be assembled for a two-week team training exercise during which their team and SAP skills will be tested and refined in parallel.

Each member will assume a role similar to that which is planned for your firm. Teams will be comprised of at least one person each for FI, SD, MM, and PP (and, optionally) HR, with one person chosen as project manager. During the first three days of the course, attendees will be presented with a detailed case study. During the remaining seven days, each team will strive to satisfy the business case by configuring SAP R/3. During these seven days, instructors fill the role of "enlightened" clients, offering guidance in terms of the business case but not detailed instruction as in phase 2. At the same time, your team members will be evaluated in terms of consulting skills, team skills, and SAP implementation and configuration skills.

This subsequent round of training and testing may not be feasible for smaller firms. It should be noted, however, that all newly-hired SAP America consultants receive a ten-week course program that culminates in just such an exercise, during which inferior consultants are weeded out and only consultants with rounded skills move on.

Skills Migration for IS Staff

Your Information Systems people will find themselves in an uncomfortable position. On the one hand, they will have to keep legacy systems running while R/3 is being implemented. On the other hand, once R/3 is in place, their reason for being in your midst will largely disappear. In this light alone, converting your IS staff to SAPness is of special import.

As mentioned earlier, key skill areas for technical IS staff are Basis and ABAP/4. The position of analyst is no longer viable because no such bridge from business user to guts-of-system is required.

Another new technical horizon is the client/server itself, the maintenance of which will require expertise in networks, communications, and Basis.

Adds Nancy Bancroft, "I know of one company who outsourced all their legacy systems. Then they trained their in-house staff in SAP in preparation for their implementation project. As they have eliminated legacy systems, they have reduced the cost from the outside firm. Of course, this only works when you have planned to convert entirely to SAP, but I thought it was a good approach."

End User Training

This training, which ideally will occur just before R/3 is put into play, can be accomplished in a variety of ways, including:

Super User Model, in which designated users are fully trained by the project team members and then pass on that training to their cohorts.

Project Team, in which module specialists are responsible for the training of their relevant user groups.

Outsourced Training, in which end user training specialists use project documentation as a basis for training of user groups.

There are no absolute methods that must be followed for end user training. These methods are often mixed to the advantage of a project. For example, outsourcing is chosen but project team members are also involved as is a super user so that project team members provide R/3 context, super users provide end business use context and credibility, and the outsourcing specialist provides techniques and experience for the creation of training materials.

Method	Advantage	Disadvantage
Super User	The user group takes responsibility for making it all work.	Hard to ID a super user; super users do not always know the answer to 'why?'
Project Team	Can answer the question 'why?'.	Not empathetic to user group concerns; maintains responsibility at project team level
Outsource	Training specialists are on the scene	Lack of project context

Note that the standard method for creating core end user training materials is to take key documents created in the TO BE phase, such as process scripts and convert them from specifications to guides.

The Cost of SAP Education

Management Training

There are a variety of management seminars and overview classes available and although the quality of these courses will vary wildly, the costs are generally in the range of $500-$750 per participant, excluding expenses.

Small firms may find it feasible to send a management group to an open seminar but larger firms will almost certainly prefer to have the seminars given *in situ*. Again, gathering executives for even a single day is a difficult enough task; sending them collectively on the road may prove impossible.

Project Team Training

Count on $15-$20K per team member, plus expenses. This includes an overview/SAP business seminar (~$1K), a two-week horizontal/integration exercise (~$5K), three to four weeks of SAP America product training (~$10K), and one week of field training (~$2K). Expenses will be incurred as well.

End Users

Whichever method you choose, you will spend between $400 and $700 per user. Because such training usually takes place on site, expenses should be minor.

Overall, your SAP education costs should come to about 10% of the entire costs of the endeavor. If this total, or any of the other sub-amounts, seems high to you, just read on.

The Cost of Lousy Training

A pro football team practices (i.e., the players are taught and go through endless rehearsals) from mid-July until the first week of

September before playing a first game. Why? Because the coaches want to win. Imagine what would happen if the players just showed up about a week before the first game, were offered a motivational slide show, and handed a manual outlining the plays? (Actually, I think the New York Jets tried this for a few years and the results weren't pretty.)

On the other hand, what would happen if players chose the training they wanted (for their own career path) and did not practice together?

For years, education budgets were viewed more as employee benefits rather than as beneficial to the company itself, as in "We're investing a lot in your future, Jenkins. Don't let us down." And Jenkins was allowed to choose a course or seminar each year or so in order to expand his professional repertoire.

Happily, companies have changed their outlook and employee education is an integral part of any working day. The 'Japan Panic' of the 1980's played a large part because Japanese dominance in that decade was viewed as heavily due to their enlightened policies of employee training.

Still, when it comes to what many still view as a 'computer project', SAP education budgets are more often on the skinny side of what is truly called for.. Project managers are always under the gun about budgets and education is an easy target for cutting corners. So, ok, go ahead and whittle those education costs to the bone. Here is what you get in return for those savings slivers:

Captain, My Captain

In the late 1970's, intent upon modernizing their country, the Saudi Arabian Royal Government ordered millions of dollars worth of IBM computers. The hardware was duly delivered and installed but, to the chagrin of the Saudis, it did not work. Um, there was no, uh, software. It seems that the Saudi senior executives were not particularly well-informed.

The savings of management education are simple to grasp but difficult to quantify.

If your leaders think of R/3 as their downsizing buddy, and guide the project accordingly, how many thousands of dollars are lost in the venture and how many hearts broken?

If your leaders think of R/3 as only some hot new software, how much money will be wasted while they resist the organizational changes that are conjured by an R/3 installation?

If your leaders ignore the meaning of the project and simply throw a lot of money at consultants to "put it in", how much will that cost and to what benefit?

Pay the Trainer or Pay the Consultant More

The average cost of an experienced R/3 consultant is $150 per hour, or $24,000 per month plus expenses.

The average cost of an internal project member (inexperienced in SAP, but experienced in your business) is less than half the amount of the external consultant.

The table below illustrates the difference in cost for internal and

Internal Staff		
	Monthly	6 Months
Salary & benefits	$8,333	$50,000
SAP Education @$20K	$3,333	$20,000
Total Cost	$11,667	$70,000
External Consultant		
	Monthly	6 Months
Fees ($150 per hr x 160)	$24,000	$144,000
Expenses (15% of fees)	$3,600	$21,600
	$27,600	$165,600
Difference	$(15,933)	$(95,600)

external consultants, including a $20K investment in education for the internal consultants.

Clearly, you cannot entirely replace the need for outside consulting with SAP education, but you can hasten the departure of consultants by investing in your own people. This is simple enough to understand only if you clearly grasp the principle that an R/3 implementation is a business project rather than an information systems project.

An even simpler yardstick is to consider that the $20K investment you make for education is the equivalent of less than one month of outside consulting. Multiply these figures by the number of team members and the number of months called for in your project plan.

The potential downside to this investment in education is that you may also hasten the departure of your internal staff to the wild west of SAP consulting. As previously mentioned, you risk losing about one third of your staff. This loss, however, does not offset the obvious gains that SAP education will afford you.

The Cost of Looking It Up

Knowledgeable, well-educated users will still, on occasion, have to refer to help guides or help desks for directions in system use. Poorly educated users will regularly be referring to help guides or help desks for directions in system use. How much does this look-up time cost your company? If the look up takes the form of "Alice, how the hell do I post an invoice in French francs?", then both the looker upper and Alice are involved, doubling the lost time. And if the look-up is at a crucial juncture and results in a loss of business, tote that up, too.

A good analogy might be to consider how much time it takes someone to drive from home to a hospital five miles away as opposed to the time it takes a business traveler, using a roadmap as a guide, to drive from a hotel to a hospital five miles away. In short, you arrive more surely at your destination if you know the way in advance.

Since we are mixing metaphors here, let us go back to the analogy of the football team: after that first game is won or lost, and for every week between subsequent games, the football team is back in practice, still learning, still rehearsing. By the same token, end user training will have to be refreshed and repeated on occasion, for both rookies and veterans, according to wins and losses.

In her book *SAP Documentation & Training, A Development Guide*, (BobKat Press, 1997) Kathryn Park offers a detailed table of the cost of users (in the midst of business) having to stop and look up directions for system use. Her premise is that an employee being paid $50,000 a year is therefore costing 7 cents per second. Looking at a fairly conservative scenario, a poorly trained end user will have to 'look it up' about ten times a day and each look-up may take 20 or more seconds. With 200 work days, the company is losing around $400 a year per user.

This strikes me as an ultraconservative estimate. You be the judge.

More and more companies are focused on post-implementation supports such as Help Desk and online documentation. Others are all het up about Computer Based Training (CBT), which is costly and provides nothing in the way of give and take. Although the potential value of these supports is without question, we find that greater and more lasting value will come from solid, upfront user training with a live teacher, a motivated set of students, and sufficient training supports to save the day.

CHAPTER 6

The Cost of the Journey

◻ Now We Know Better

◻ Predictable Costs 1: Software

◻ Predictable Costs 2: Hardware

◻ Estimating Software and Hardware Costs

◻ Consulting Costs and How to Control Them

◻ Budget Modeling for SAP Implementations

◻ Executive Oversight and the High Cost of SAP

◻ Post Script: SAP, Showgirls, and the Chicago Cubs

The Cost of the Journey

Now We Know Better

A few years after R/3 was announced, we began to see articles in the press about the high cost of SAP. Two elements were regularly cited as the fault: 1) the length of implementation time and 2) the high levels of consulting required. Often, these press reports were fair-minded and incisive, but just as often they were shrill and off the mark. Many companies had labored to implement and found themselves well short of success…and so blamed the supplier and the consultants. In the majority of these cases, the failures originated on the home front, but both SAP and the consulting world played their part.

Time has passed and the lessons of 1992-1996 have led to serious changes to the consulting ranks and to the philosophy (or methodology) of implementing.. This chapter provides a concise summary of those lessons.

There are four levels of costs involved in the acquisition and implementation of SAP software:

1.   The software license

2. The associated hardware
3. Consulting (internal & external)
4. Education & Change Management

The first two of these elements are more measurable, more predictable, and more easily controlled than the second two.

Since cost is as much an emotional issue as a business issue, it is important to establish *realistic* expectations. We already know that most software initiatives are 'late' and 'over budget', but we also know that project plans and budgets for those projects are seldom reality-based and, more likely, founded on good intentions.

Below is a chart of what most firms target for cost distribution for SAP implementations as opposed to the reality of where the money goes.

	Target	Reality
SAP Education & Change Mgmt	10%	5%
Hardware & License	33%	20%
Consulting	33%	45%
Other (interfacing, change mgmt, add-on software)	24%	30%

The 'reality' figures are not particularly acceptable and we are not suggesting you should emulate them. The amount spent for education should be higher. If it is, as will be elaborated in a later chapter, the amount spent for consulting will decline proportionally.

Predictable Costs 1: Software

SAP software is acquired in the form of a license. Though variations exist (and these variations often depend upon your negotiations with SAP), the license elements include:

⅃ The number of users, which may be broken down by types

of users (end users, occasional users, etc.)

⌐ The type of license being issued, whether for a single site or multiple sites, for global use, etc.

⌐ The number of modules chosen

⌐ The number of instances (concurrent versions of the software) required.

SAP prides itself on the fact that its product can be successful in a wide variety of industry sectors and has proven to be somewhat liberal in its price breaks when clients find ways to identify themselves as 'beta' sites, meaning the first of a given kind. A price break may also be given if your firm has a high profile of some sort and the publicity resulting from your license will be favorable to SAP.

Since we are on the subject of cost, you should be aware of the fact that during the licensing negotiations, you may be given the impression from SAP that license costs will represent roughly one third of your over-all investment. This may or may not be the case. Traditional software projects were said to have a two-to-one ratio of consulting costs over software/hardware. As has been demonstrated, SAP endeavors do not follow tradition.

Such a ratio may exist for you if you implement according to the Accelerated SAP methodology, but please review our subchapter on this subject before raising your expectations too high.

Predictable Costs 2: Hardware

Whether the platform supplier you choose is IBM, Hewlett Packard, Digital Equipment, or any other is of no major import to hardware costs unless you are made a special offer.

What more directly determines hardware costs is the size and complexity of your physical plant. If your users are all huddled under one roof, your costs will obviously be less than if they are scattered across multiple sites.

Another key cost factor will be whether or not you use the full three-tier client/server architecture or opt for a simpler two-tier set-up. Large firms often find the need for multiple R/3's which can lead to additional hardware. Smaller firms, satisfied with a single R/3 installation, can more easily envision a single two-tier client/server.

Despite the fact that hardware costs are fairly predictable, they will vary from your original estimates once R/3 is functioning. The network will have to be tuned and re-tuned according to volume and traffic. R/3 is vast and deep and requires some fairly serious horsepower to do its magic.

Estimating Software and Hardware Costs

Getting an estimate on direct costs is simpler than you might think.

A basic cost yardstick is as follows:

Per user, per module = $2,000 license fee.

Thus, if your firm has 100 users working on a reasonable three-tier network and you are licensing FI, CO, SD, MM, and PP, your license and hardware will come to about $1M (100 x (5 x 2000)).

These costs are pretty much fifty-fifty, but will be driven up or down primarily by hardware considerations rather than SAP licensing.

Consulting Costs and How to Control Them

This sub-chapter addresses the costs of consulting help for SAP endeavors, and will only be fully understood if studied in the context of our preceding chapter on SAP consulting.

As mentioned earlier, in traditional systems projects, consulting costs were generally twice the total of hardware and software costs. In the history of SAP implementations in North America, the ratio for most projects has been in the neighborhood three or four or even five to one. Some of the reasons for this are linked to the critical differences between SAP endeavors and traditional implementations:

⅃ SAP embraces the entire enterprise, thus adding complexity when compared to projects that only address limited segments of an enterprise.

⅃ SAP invites business process reengineering, which is both complex and time-consuming

⅃ SAP is implemented by teams of business people, not built in the white tower of an IS shop. There are more players on the field.

These are natural and understandable cost factors that lead to higher consulting costs. However, there is one other factor that is (perhaps) natural and (sigh) understandable which has played a larger part in sometimes excessive consulting costs: incompetence.

Some of you are already applauding, certain as you have always been that consultants are a race of greedy charlatans, but the incompetence sword cuts both ways and, *caveat emptor,* the consultants are only the hired hands.

But before we brood over consulting incompetence, let's take a look at the prevailing rates.

Daily Costs	Free-lance	Consulting Firm	Internal*
Senior Consultant	NA	$2500-$3500	NA
Project Manager	$1500-$2000	$2000-$2500	$700-$900
Team Leader	$1200-$1800	$1600-$2000	$500-$800
Module Consultant	$1000-$1500	$1200-$1700	$300-$500
Basis Administration	$1000-$1500	$1200-$2000	NA
Basis Consultant	$ 900-$1500	$1200-$1700	NA
ABAP Engineer	$ 800-$1200	$ 800-$1400	NA
ABAP Programmer	$ 500-$1000	$ 800-$1000	NA

* the cost of internal consultants is based upon assumed salary ranges of $120K-$150K for a project manager, $80K to $100K for a team leader, and $50K-$80K for a module consultant. The cost includes benefits and other employee-rated overheads and is included here to illustrate the point that internal consulting is not free.

Although you may find a way to engage SAP consultants for lower rates than those noted here, you will get better cost-savings results if you master the time spent by consultants and shorten the duration of their stay. This is an area where, in the recent past, client incompetence was fairly rampant. "Only a wise prince can be wisely advised," warned Machiavelli, and not all of the corporate princes out there have taken heed. Firms engaging SAP consultants have repeatedly made the following mistakes:

1. Failing to confirm SAP experience. By engaging a consulting firm but not screening the individual consultants proposed, clients have left themselves exposed to many of the tricks detailed in our chapter on 'The Wild West of SAP Consulting.'

2. Leaving it to the experts. When consultants lead the project and perform the key tasks (such as module configuring) rather than stressing transfer of SAP knowledge, they risk harboring consultants longer than is necessary. Further

damage is caused to the esteem of employees who find themselves on the periphery of the project rather than at the core.

3. Assuming that SAP is a technical matter. By hiring or assigning good IS people rather than good business people, (thus treating the project like a traditional IS project) clients tend to follow project methodologies that are inefficient for R/3 implementations.

4. Allowing consultants to manage project scope. Initially, the consultants know more about SAP than does the client and fulfill the role of scout. As the project continues, there will be sufficient temptation to enlarge the scope. Some (but not all) consultants will take advantage of this in order to extend their stay or to add additional consulting resource. Final decisions about scope should be made by client management.

5. The Chinese Army approach. When projects are falling behind in terms of deadlines, some clients throw additional consulting resource into the fray in a vain attempt to catch up. Too many people configuring the same module creates conflict that will hinder progress rather than speed it up.

6. Lack of orientation/direction. Project team members who are there at the beginning of a project are usually clued in as to project objectives, scope, the vision, etc. Consultants who are later brought in often find themselves inserted into ongoing projects without so much as a one-day orientation. The erroneous assumption is that the consultant knows SAP and so of course will know exactly what to do.

It is difficult, but by no means impossible, to find the right SAP consultants at the right time for your endeavor. Having them around is only a part of the challenge.

While you head home at 6 PM, they tend to hang (especially on Tuesday, Wednesday and Thursday) the extra hour or two to fulfill their obligations, and then they wander back to the Holiradihiltonyatt for a night of club sandwich, a quick phone call home, e-mail and Spectravision. (Note that travelling SAP consultants tend to work in pyramids. Monday 5 hours and Friday 5 hours, with Wed-Thur totalling 35 or more.) When you notice on a Friday at 3:30 that your SD-MM specialist may not be there, remember that this person may not return home until 10 PM or later on Fridays and awaken at an hour in the very low single digits each Monday just to get back to the job by 10 AM or so. SAP . . . suitcase and passport.

Consultants should be treated as partners, not mercenaries. Most of the time, they are travelling to the client site, spending their nights in hotels, and flying home for weekends only. They should best be used a guides, teachers, and pathfinders, not as the primary builders of a client's R/3 infra-structural support.

If they fail to shorten your learning curve, something is wrong in the process. As we said earlier, the consultants are the *hired hands*. You do the hiring; you are responsible.

Indy, They've Taken the Children From the Village!

In the 1980's, SAP AG instituted an ABAP program in India and created the first ABAP/4 factory. In years since, hundreds of Indian nationals with ABAP/4 skills have sought work in other countries, most notably in the United States. Given the shortage of SAP consultants, work visas for SAPeers are relatively easy to obtain.

By consequence, since mid-1996 there has been a market glut for ABAP help. This glut has driven the cost of ABAP/4 programming downward, in direct contrast to the other SAP areas. It is not only Indian nationals who are causing this glut; the perception is that ABAP/4 skills will give one an entry into other SAP consulting, and new hundreds of North Americans are claiming ABAP/4 skills as well.

The field is not as easy to read as it was some years ago. There is now a split between experienced software engineers (most of them certified in ABAP/4, many of them Indian) and the very many -Indian, North American, Asian, and European- who quite simply have learned ABAP/4 programming.

When engaging outside ABAP/4 help, you should clearly determine what level of help you need. Some ABAP/4 people have serious experience within specific modules and will be well worth a higher rate than someone who has merely learned to write code.

In this same vein, a number of SAP consulting firms offer 'ABAP factory' supports, usually overseas. Their lure is cheap ABAP customization and the shine to that lure usually is in the form of easy transmission of specifications from your site to the 'factory' and back. Treat such firms as you would treat the plague. Heavy customization of your R/3 will chain you to these firms forever. You will not be able to upgrade your R/3 to newer SAP offerings without also updating all of the keen modifications that these firms will have made for you. In essence, such customization turns configurable software into the same old program mode of traditional (read: old-fashioned) systems. The bottom line: ABAP factories are a racket and nothing more.

Budget Modeling for SAP Implementations

Attempting to anticipate the cost of a project can be perilous, particularly if the project success is going to be judged in accordance with your adherence to a budget.

At the same time, it is not an exercise that requires sophisticated costing software and untold hours of data gymnastics. The last thing you want to do is use project management planning software that includes "rates" for project team members and provides "costs" by activity, phase, task, and all the rest. You will preferably use such software for budgetary and planning control, not as a master plan cost estimate.

In the model we propose, there are three layers of costs:

⌐ Direct Costs: hardware and software

⌐ Indirect Costs: primarily consulting, both internal & external

⌐ Education: including the levels described in the education chapter of this book.

As noted earlier, the direct costs will be about $2,000 per user, per module.

For an estimate of indirect costs, more soul-searching is required than numbers crunching. The normal duration of the activities of an SAP R/3 implementation are fairly well known. What matters are the conditions in which the project will be carried out. These conditions can be more difficult to measure, but again, not as difficult as you may think.

This budget model uses weighted scores in order to determine what multiple of your direct costs will be needed for indirect costs. The elements of your own company to be measured are:

1. Sites/complexity. How many operational sites will be included in the core implementation? The working definition of 'operational sites' is the number of different physical locations where a significant number of workstations will be in use.

2. Level of business process reengineering envisioned. As we have seen, some implementations (of the ASAP variety) limit the amount of business process reengineering to be

accomplished as part of the core implementation. Assign a weight between 1 (very little or none) to 5 (across the board changes) depending upon the level you anticipate.

3. Legacy systems retained. Each legacy application that you will retain adds weight to a degree of 10%.

4. Staff readiness and management commitment are the final two elements and are scored from 1 (strong) to 5 (weak). These are the most difficult to measure if you have your head in the clouds and easy enough to measure if you take a hard look at reality. In the SAP Back Pages chapter of this book is a subsection concerning company readiness for SAP that may help you in this regard. Further, one person's input of a score for these elements may not be sufficient. Just as some Olympics gymnastics judges never score a performance a 10 on principal, the variances of subjective scoring can be important. In companies where this weighting system has been applied, different individuals have filled out the scores and culminated these weights into a consensus average.

Because small firms are built differently, and certainly managed differently than are large firms, the weights vary for the two groups. Business process reengineering, for example, is far more simply applied in small firms than in behemoths. Senior management is more visible and hands-on in smaller firms, so the commitment weighting for them and for general staff is higher than in large firms.

Fiddling with these rates is acceptable, but the results will still be about the same.

Indirect Cost Element	Small <$500M	Mid-Large >$500M
Sites	5%	10%
BPR Level	15%	25%
Legacy Systems	10%	10%
Staff Readiness	30%	20%
Mgt Commitment	40%	35%

This modeling method has been met with some skepticism by people who have already developed implementation budgets in the traditional fashion. Their estimates tend to be about 60% of the total that this model yields. The variance can be found in the distinctions between SAP and tradition. Any project cost estimate that does not take these distinctions into account will result in a project that is late and over budget the day it begins.

				Small/Mid-sized Firm
Direct Costs		$2,000		per user per module licensed
Number of users		50		
Number of modules		5		
			$500,000	Hardware/software
Indirect Cost Factors	*Nbr/Score*	*Weight*	*Multiplier*	*Comments*
Sites/complexity	2	5%	0.10	Number of operational sites
Level of BPR	2	15%	0.30	1=none, 5=radical change
Legacy systems	3	10%	0.30	Nbr of systems to be interfaced
Staff Readiness	3	30%	0.90	1=eager 5=resisting
Mgmt Commitment	2	40%	0.80	1=full 5=shaky
		100%	2.40	**indirect cost multiplier**
Indirect Cost	$500,000	2.40	$1,200,000	(Direct costs x indirect factor)
Sub-total			$1,700,000	(Direct costs + indirect costs)
SAP Education		10%	$170,000	
Total Estimate			**$1,870,000**	

This firm has two operational sites, plans to perform a minimum of business process reengineering, and will retain three of its legacy systems. Management is fairly strongly committed to the project, but staff readiness has not yet followed this commitment.

With 50 users and five modules being licensed, the direct costs come to $500,000. The indirect cost multiplier is 2.4 so indirect costs will be $1.2M. Tack on 10% for training and the total cost estimate is $1,870,000.

				Large Firm
Direct Costs	$2,000			per user per module licensed
Number of users	300			
Number of modules	5			
Total Direct Costs		$3,000,000		**Hardware/software**
Indirect Cost Factors	Nbr/Score	Weight	Multiplier	Comments
Sites/complexity	4	10%	0.40	Number of operational sites
Level of BPR	3	25%	0.75	1=none, 5=radical change
Legacy systems	3	10%	0.30	Nbr of systems to be interfaced
Staff Readiness	3	20%	0.60	1=eager 5=resisting
Mgmt Commitment	3	35%	1.05	1=full 5=shaky
		100%	**3.10**	**indirect cost multiplier**
Indirect Cost	$3,000,000	3.10	$9,300,000	(Direct costs x indirect factor)
Sub-total			$12,300,000	(Direct costs + indirect costs)
SAP Education		10%	$1,230,000	
Total Estimate			**$13,530,000**	

This firm has four operational sites, plans on median-level business processing reengineering, and will retain three legacy systems. Management commitment is lukewarm and this commitment is reflected by general staff.

With 300 users and five modules licensed, the direct cost estimate is $3M. The indirect cost multiplier is 3.1 so the estimate for indirect costs is $9.3M. With another 10% added to the sub-total for education, the total budget estimate is $13,530,000.

As an example of the savings that upfront SAP education can bring, this estimate would drop to $12,870,000 if staff readiness improved to a 2. If management commitment followed suit, the estimate would drop to $11,715,000, a net savings of $1,815,000.

You don't believe me? You prefer to just dive into the fray and make sparks fly without upfront education? Go ahead, make my day.

Executive Oversight and the High Cost of SAP

In the late 1980's, when the Hunt brothers were accused of seeking to corner the global silver market, Nelson Hunt told the members of a congressional hearing that "a billion dollars isn't what it used to be". In the realm of SAP implementations, there is a similar sentiment, that ten million dollars or thirty million or fifty million isn't what it used to be. Fortune 500 firms, rushing to acquire and implement SAP R/3, are finding that the price tag often exceeds one hundred million dollars. In many quarters, sticker shock has led to whining and the whining has turned to outright wailing, much of it finding its way into print.

Why is it so expensive to implement SAP R/3?

As Mr. Hunt explained, expense is relative. With SAP, companies can envision global implementations, with rollouts that take three to four years. Proctor & Gamble, Bristol-Myers Squibb, Dupont, Saturn, and Hercules are just a few of the companies that have already implemented a core of R/3 and are in the midst of continuing implementation and global roll-out. In many quarters, this length of time is viewed as excessive. Senior managers often fail to understand that SAP implementations are enterprise-wide and should not be compared to previous, traditional implementations of software, nearly all of which were limited to one or two business segments, such as finance and accounting or sales and distribution.

All the same, senior management tends to measure SAP costs *in relation to previous IS projects*. They fail to grasp that implementing SAP is a business project, not an IS project. Furthermore, it is enterprise-wide, so the stakes are higher, the players far more numerous, and the changes engendered far-reaching. This is not apples to oranges; it is more like olives to watermelons.

The fact of the matter is that there is no benchmark for the duration of SAP implementations. No such projects had ever been undertaken before the arrival of R/3.

COST DRIVERS IN AN SAP IMPLEMENTATION

DRIVER	EFFECT
Premature Gap Analysis	Pointless ABAP/4 Customization
Management Misconceptions	Project Stop and Re-start
Poor SAP Knowledge Transfer	Addiction to Consultants
Use of Traditional IS Benchmarks	Misplaced Expectations

Secondly, as we have already noted, the costs of hardware and licensing may come to only 25% of the overall price tag. SAP implementations are almost invariably coupled with reengineering efforts which drive the costs higher and the timeline into years. All of these cash outlays are then bundled into 'the high cost of SAP' rather than 'the high cost of re-inventing your corporation, managing the enormous change that this implies, and implementing software to support that re-invention.'

Most often cited is the high cost of consulting. Yes, SAP consulting is definitely at a premium, but clients hurt themselves even more by not making good use of that consulting. Failing to understand SAP at the beginning of a project, the majority of clients tend to let the consultants lead the implementation rather than guide it. SAP training afforded to client staff is usually limited to module training and continues to represent less than 5% of most budgets. This failure of knowledge transfer leaves most clients addicted to their consultants. This addiction is costly and gets chalked up to SAP rather than to poor project management as should be the case.

[The] failure of knowledge transfer leaves most clients addicted to their consultants. This addiction is costly and gets chalked up to SAP rather than to poor project management...

What contributes most to the high cost of SAP is the cycle of false starts and re-starts. An inability to reach the finish line has been noted in many North American SAP implementations. This inability is usually due to a lack of upfront understanding of what SAP is all about. Following the Nike method of implementation (Just Do It), clients pour their resources into rapid configuration of SAP, while ignoring the business side of the undertaking.

Says Nancy Bancroft, "You will change your business when you implement SAP because the software itself will require new ways of operating. It makes sense then to initiate a business process redesign effort in the context of SAP in order to make such changes thoughtfully. If you simply let the people doing the configuration of the system make those decisions, some will be detrimental to your business process."

Consider this Seven Act Tragedy which has been performed around the world in countless corporate theaters:

Act I: We Know What We're Doing Here

The company acquires SAP R/3 and thinks of it as the hot new software, only slightly different from software acquired in the past; in parallel, a traditional software methodology is adopted.

Act II: The University of Us

Consultants, both internal and external, get lost in the AS-IS and TO-BE phases which comprise Business Process Reengineering.

Act III: Clowns to the Left of Me, Jokers to the Right

Inexperienced project members cannot match SAP functionality to their TO-BE vision. Elements that are assumed to be missing are listed in a 'Gap analysis'.

Act IV: A Nip Here, a Tuck There

In order to fill the gaps, unnecessary add-on software is purchased and unnecessary customization of R/3 occurs. The timeline and budget are revised and expanded. Fistfights are imminent. Consultants cease traveling the hallways alone.

Act V: I Think She's Got It!

As time passes inexperience with R/3 turns to experience. The project team receives additional training. The gap analysis is revised, and there is a visible turnover of outside consultants. The traditional implementation methodology is updated to address enterprise-wide and highly-integrated elements of R/3 that were previously ignored.

Act VI: Starting Over

New business process reengineering is begun in mid-project, but battle fatigue has set in and the vision is no longer to seize potentials benefits but to finish the damned project.

Act VII: Obituary

Angry articles are written about the high cost of SAP.

This tragedy can be easily avoided if the education that tends to occur in Act V would be undertaken between Acts I and 2. The result would be neither comedy nor love story, but there would be a lot less violence.

Post Script - SAP, Showgirls, and the Chicago Cubs

In any study of the costs of a business initiative, we find that the concept turns back upon itself unless benefits are included in the equation. Clearly, you will not want to invest millions of dollars and thousands of employee hours only to find your company in the same state in which you are today. You are choosing to implement SAP because you want to seize the benefits of having an integrated suite of applications that will provide a foundation for workflow, the reduction of work (ergo, costs), and a radically improved service to customers.

There is no success inherent to 'finishing.' Every year the Chicago Cubs finish the season. The movie 'Showgirls' came to an end with no visible benefit to anyone. In the midst of most SAP implementations, the notion of benefits gets lost in the gunsmoke and din of battle. Costs are high and energy lagging. You are trying to so hard to "finish" that the reasons behind the venture get mislaid. Put the accent of achieving benefits for cost, not just on cost alone.

CHAPTER 7

Hearts, Minds, Pink Slips, & Career Paths

⌐ Throwing Yourself on the SAP Sword

⌐ Communicating Change

⌐ We Had a Meeting and You Weren't There

Hearts, Minds, Pink Slips, & Career Paths

Throwing Yourself on the SAP Sword

You have been a member of your firm for more than seven years and although you have not ascended the ranks with lightning speed, you nonetheless have seen a clear career path before you. Three times in the past four years, you have worked as a team leader on special initiatives and you pride yourself on your broad vision of the company rather than settling on simply mastering your current position.

Over a period of a few months, you hear rumblings that your company may acquire and implement SAP. Within weeks, the rumor mill is in full gear but you seek to remain above it, to consider the possibility of a major project with a cool perspective.

One day, a consultant five years younger than you appears on the scene. She bears a binder packed with charts and when she unfolds her laptop, it displays a series of color slides that make only vague sense to you. All the same, you are interested and her answers to your questions only heighten your interest. Some weeks later, when you understand that an implementation team is being formed internally, you volunteer to join it on condition that, at project's end, you may return to your old job.

You receive SAP training and participate in the planning process. Later, as a last step before configuring SAP, your task is to reconsider all that is done in your old department within the context of the entire enterprise. Initial improvements that are suggested begin to unravel into major improvements of surprising scope and dramatic benefit. One element of these improvements is a flattening of your staff chart. Within that flattening is the disappearance of your job.

This scenario has already been repeated hundreds of times throughout the SAP world and will continue to be a 'continent' on the change management map.

A venture into SAP and, more to the point, business process reengineering, will at first produce confusion and anxiety within the employee populace. If change management is a part of your project, that confusion can be turned to understanding and the anxiety honestly addressed. If change management is *not* a part of your project, confusion will flower into bewilderment and anxiety into rage. With reason.

As new business processes are contemplated, old jobs are placed into limbo, new jobs are ill-defined, turf is eliminated, habits are broken, traditions are trampled, some people are absent and others have survival guilt, past skills are no longer honored, and training for necessary new skills is hard to find. Worse, there are highly-paid consultants wandering the hallways, current business is suffering because of the time sucked up by the SAP project, and there is a deadline hanging over everyone's head like the sword of Damocles.

Who wants to work here?

This is not a worst case scenario; it is reflection of some of the many firms that have lived through just such an environmental hazard. In most of these cases, R/3 was finally implemented and did bring benefit to the firm, but at a cost to the employees that was both unnecessary and cruel because the human element of the SAP project was ignored.

We already know that business organizations are not democracies, just as we know that our primary business function is to bring profits to stockholders. We also recognize that any project intended to be of benefit *to the company* may not be of benefit to each and every individual in that company. There will be losers, and they will not necessarily be of the 'dead wood' variety that needed to be swept away.

A venture into enterprise renewal of this scope can be liberating. Jobs that seemed destined for Dilbertville can be traded for jobs that adhere to exciting horizons, new skills, and an improved company identity. Pointless activities can be replaced by value-added activities that bring more profits to both shareholders and employees alike. Such a scenario has also resulted from an R/3 implementation project. The difference between this scenario and the previous may simply lie in diverse company cultures. I have been in consulting for over fifteen years and have spent considerable amounts of time at over thirty different clients. At some clients, you can feel the sunshine; at others, you just smell the burning.

All the same, company culture is only one element that determines the humanitarian level of an SAP venture. Change management, and how it is applied, covers most of the others.

Communicating Change

Common wisdom says that people are naturally resistant to change. This is scarcely precise. People are naturally resistant to blind change or to change that is thrust upon them without explanation or justification.

Not everything about the unknown is frightening. If your office is in basement C, just past the boiler room and kitty corner to the rubbish haul, and you are told that you are changing offices, will that make you afraid? Wouldn't you imagine that wherever you are going has to be better? But if you occupy a corner office on the 33rd floor, just down the hall from the CEO and with a stunning view of the city, and are told you are changing offices, you will undoubtedly feel threatened *until the destination of the move is revealed to you.*

Revealing the destination of an SAP undertaking to the employee mass is not a one-shot affair. At the outset, the destination (or vision) will necessarily be more difficult to describe than it will be once project development is well under way. Further, by virtue of the scope of such an undertaking (enterprise-wide) there will be visible shifts in the destination, and these will have to be communicated throughout the duration of the exercise.

The following are useful means of describing the destination to the employee body:

Project Charter

The content and purpose of this document are covered in Chapter 3: SAP in a Microwave.

Newsletter

On a monthly basis, a newsletter should be posted or generally distributed. This letter should include basic project news such as the announcement of new people in project roles or the installation of screens in a given department. The tone and content of the newsletter should reflect the reality of the project. It is acceptable to describe hurdles and obstacles and to solicit suggestions. This newsletter is not 'Pravda' and it should not be used to propagandize to the people who will genuinely care about how the project is going.

Bulletins

As you come to specific milestones for specific areas of the business, bulletins can be distributed to affected personnel in order to prepare them.

For example, if you are about to launch the drafting of new procedures for sales order processing, the bulletin would be addressed to everyone in the order fulfillment process. Bulletin content might include charts and scripts of intended sub-processes, some explanatory text, and some comment about the importance of the new procedures. Once the procedures have been drafted, they may form the base content for a subsequent bulletin.

The point is to communicate what you are cooking while you are cooking it, so your audience does not find itself faced with an enchilada to digest when all they expected was a tossed salad.

Town Hall Meetings

Executive presence speaks volumes, as does executive absence. If your firm has executives who a) understand the venture and b) can express the purpose of it, it would be wise to send them out for periodic town hall meetings. These consist of 15-20 minute visits to various company departments to present the project, justify its aims, and take questions.

The mere experience of hearing executives talking about the project provides credibility and underscores your purpose. On the other hand, executives need to hear the feedback of employees on the same subject.

'Communication is the key' is the most meaningless of terms if it is applied with a shrug or as a chore. If you have executives who quite simply are not communicators, this may not be the right idea. What matters is that you fill the vacuum between executive intent and employee understanding of that intent. This is true even if the message is not particularly welcome.

What it boils down to is the difference between these reactions:

⌐ I didn't hear you say anything so I don't know what you believe.

⌐ I heard what you said and I agree/disagree but I appreciate knowing what you believe.

Open House (Prototype Demos and Rehearsals)

The best way to sell the SAP project is to let it sell itself, by demonstration, to all those who need to see it in action.

Once a viable prototype is available, key staff from each of your business areas should be brought in and given a walk-through of how R/3 will help to fulfill the new business processes. Live ammo (real data) is preferable to blanks (made up test data) because some people have a hard time extrapolating.

The "show me" attitude is one that will prevail, most particularly when you are dealing with people who will have to *touch* the system on a daily basis. A live walk-through will do absolute wonders toward breaking down resistance and gathering enthusiasm for the venture. By the same token, a poorly-prepared walk-through will be disastrous. Be sure that your floor show is ready to go before opening the curtain or you risk losing your immediate audience and the resulting bad word of mouth will spread faster than rumors about dicey presidential behavior.

Listening to the Nay-Sayers

Acceptance of change will never be universal or complete, especially in the North American culture, where individuality is encouraged. Your firm will have its share of nay sayers, people who resist the change, resist R/3, or simply resist you. If your response to resistance is to merely squash it, you will probably fail. There is as more wisdom in intelligent resistance than in blind obedience and often the resistance will spring from a just source.

For example, a troop of consultants descended upon a Fortune 500 firm and quickly put their implementation methodology into play. This methodology included a detailed "AS IS" phase that quickly sucked up many valuable hours, both on the client side and on the consulting side. A number of the client staff resisted the effort, finding it pointless, but were told by project management and executive staff to buckle under. These people grew to resent not only the AS IS exercise but the consultants and, by extension, the whole project. This resistance soon spread throughout the firm's many divisions and was a major element of the project's final collapse. (As it happens, this company was a veritable laboratory of SAP failure, where a nine-figure investment over three years yielded little more than rage, a thousand sad anecdotes, and the massive circulation of resumes.)

In this case, the nay sayers were right and their resistance should have been cautionary.

By the same token, some people will take the 'over my dead body' stance. For these people, your choice of candlestick, wrench, rope, or pink slip will be a matter of personal style.

We Had a Meeting and You Weren't There

>Gold is not going to flow from an R/3 installation, only data.

I once worked in a company in which fear of being fired was a daily stimulant for most of the executives.

In this company, important decisions were announced on a Monday and forgotten by Wednesday. Deadlines for various initiatives were set and then forgotten. Bonuses were dangled, but seldom paid, partnerships were tendered but no real partnership was ever put into practice. The executive turnover was understandably high and morale was chronically low. In a business arena in which even the brain-dead were pulling a profit, this firm was unsurprisingly in the red.

What kept people working in such a hellish environment? Great expectations. When first hired, we had all been given lofty visions of what our careers would be, how we would be utilized, and what positions we would occupy. Some would become partners within a limited amount of time, others would become executive vice presidents. One would head up a soon-to-formed new division; another would 'take charge' of a newly-delineated region.

As the company lurched southward and grumbling set in, there were shake-ups, heart to hearts, new intentions, and new expectations cast across the conference table. Only the recurring realities of the place ratcheted those expectations into the dust.

An SAP undertaking holds forth immense promise, but you do not want to sell it as the great solution to all business problems. It is not a solution at all, merely an enabler to solutions. The expectations of your employees will follow their planes of labor and you should set their expectations accordingly or risk disillusionment and the resentment it can breed.

Your **IS people** will expect a career change, either by shifting their skills to SAP or by moving their feet, left right left, out the door. This will be delayed for those companies that retain a number of legacy systems, but once a core of R/3 is installed, the writing is on the wall.

End users should expect more complex work at the entry level (integration demands it) but less peripheral business, such as reporting to other departments.

Supervisors should expect more time to concentrate on exceptional business and less time running the routine business.

Middle management should expect to be reduced in numbers. This is a given. It is the way of the world and with each revolution of the earth it is more and more of a reality, with or without SAP or Baan or Peoplesoft. A major rationale for middle management is to provide inter-departmental coordination. Much of this coordination is handled via R/3's integrated, horizontal architecture. What middle management remains in the firm can expect a faster response to management initiatives and a greater availability of reliable information.

Senior management should expect a rearrangement of corporate turf based on the new horizontal view of the company. In the longer term, they should expect more organizational flexibility, improved levels of employee morale, more timely and accurate management information and, not coincidentally, a stronger bottom line. However, if senior management is left out of the education loop, no one will know what to expect.

In all fiction and cinema, the main character begins with a goal and has to overcome obstacles to reach that goal. In *great* fiction and cinema, the goals and obstacles are also there, but the main character's 'arc' always has to do with re-invention of the self. At the end, whether or not the goal is reached, the character is vastly changed; in terms of the craft, they are 're-invented.' Your staff members will have an external goal (the implementation of SAP R/3) and will be challenged by all of the obstacles we have already inventoried in this book. However, they will also necessarily have their own personal goals, and to meet them will require their individual re-inventions of self. These re-inventions will be fueled by their fears, their ambitions, and their expectations.

Setting expectations (and striving to meet them) is a responsibility that should be shared by the project management group (i.e. the project manager, executive sponsor, and the steering committee). Your success or failure in doing so will be a pivot to project success or failure.

One missing piece to all of this is that at every one of these levels you are dealing with real live people, not the fillers of job slots. Project managers, team members, end users, and senior management...everyone has a personal stake in his or her position. If you adopt the attitude of "we had a meeting and you weren't there", the project may well succeed but morale will be so low that the motivation for seizing benefits might be nil.

Chapter 8

The Life Expectancy of SAP

⌐ What's Wrong with SAP?

⌐ The Backlash Gives Birth to Team SAP

⌐ More Wives than Brigham Young

The Life Expectancy of SAP

What's Wrong with SAP?

Any company that has enjoyed such tremendous growth in such a short period of time is bound to have problems, and SAP has had its share. Most telling is the fact that, as a corporate entity, it is very thin-skinned and often takes criticism (either from clients or the press or, God save me, consultant-writers) as an attack.

Whenever SAP is said to missing something or that it fails in some area, the supplier will respond either by presuming that the source of criticism is misinformed (as in, yes we CAN do what this person says we can't) or by plastering announcements across the universe about a new and major initiative that will plug any gaps, fill any holes, and be the finger in whatever crack in whatever dike you may have. (OK, a Dutch allusion to a German company; it couldn't be helped.) Success certainly has not led to complacency, but you would like to think there might be a certain level of placidity.

Another thing about SAP that is not wrong, but should be noted: it has an accent. Not a very strong accent, but it is there nonetheless. This is not, as you may be thinking, a nationalist slur on my part. My point is that SAP America is beholden to SAP AG, and only recently has it begun to distinguish itself to the benefit of North America. In the past year alone, two important initiatives -Team SAP and the Accelerated SAP Method- have come into being and both of these are largely based upon North American concerns. Prior to 1997, there was a distinct attitude emanating from SAP AG that implementation difficulties in North America were due to the fact that people were just not following directions. This attitude was mirrored by waves of German consultants who wondered why we could not just do things the way they had in Europe. This is what I mean by, 'it has an accent'. Not everything is geared directly to North American methods of doing business.

As for the speed and volume of new announcements, SAP is often on the slippery edge of selling vaporware. A new product or tool tends not to truly exist until three or four months after it is announced as available. What SAP will do is showcase a developing product so that we in the audience can gain enthusiasm for it. At this point, the product is not complete, but by the time we react to our enthusiasm, voila! Done.

Finally, SAP has a serious shortcoming which it shares with the rest of the world: it does not have enough sound, experienced consultants or instructors to fulfill all the promises it makes.

The chronic consulting shortfall (elaborated in Chapter 4: The Wild West of SAP Consulting) leaves SAP scrambling like everyone else in search of resource to fill project or classroom rosters. The result is that SAP consultants and instructors are just as uneven in quality as the remainder of the body of consultants around North America, which fact is not publicly recognized by SAP. How could it be? This in itself is not extraordinary. However, there is also a permeating attitude emanating from the supplier, an assumption that those who work for SAP know the subject better than someone who does not.

This may be standard human nature as observed by consultants.

It has long been noticed that people working in large and important companies think of themselves as larger and more important than people working in small companies. The size! The volume! The scope! But there are signs of a softening within SAP America. The flexing and preening of the mid 1990's have diminished and the Team SAP approach is on the rise, a trend we can only pray will take root and flourish.

The Backlash Gives Birth to Team SAP

In 1993 and 1994, while SAP revenues in North America rose from $180M to over $400M, the company enjoyed something of a honeymoon period. The equivalence of a seven-year itch kicked in by mid-1995 and the screaming and hair-pulling reached a crescendo a year later as myriad articles and studies that were highly critical of SAP were to be found. The majority of the negative press had to do with the cost and time necessary to implement SAP. Other barbs had to do with what was perceived as institutional arrogance emanating from the company itself.

To counteract this negative press, SAP at first stepped up its announcements of new versions and features, but many of these announcements were premature and only added fuel to an angry fire. Still, SAP continued to sell licenses at a gallop and the criticism had no visible commercial effect.

However, beginning in early 1997, SAP began to show a friendlier face and for the first time seemed to be listening to its client constituency. Lengthy implementations were addressed with improvements to SAP tools like the Business Engineering Workbench, additional client support staff was hired and trained, the Accelerated SAP implementation method was introduced, and, finally, the concept of Team SAP was formed.

There is nothing stunning or unique about this concept in which SAP itself takes the role of "coach" while client staff, consulting staff, platform partners, and technology partners all have "positions" and "roles". What is important is that the introduction and nurturing of this concept represent a 180 degree spin in SAP's implementation philosophy. Until Team SAP arrived, SAP played a mostly passive role in implementation projects, limiting itself to pre-sales, offering referrals to implementation partners, and then observing events from a relative distance. Now playing the role of "coach", SAP America has hired hundreds of new consultants and support staff and is taking a more direct responsibility for timely and efficient implementations.

The depth of this change was witnessed at SAPphire '97 in Orlando, Florida in late August of 1997. Previous SAPphires had included a wee too much SAP chest-thumping and product announcements. This time, client considerations (especially those relative to implementations) took center stage.

The upside of Team SAP is that the supplier can referee when consultants are out of control and can play lifeguard when clients dive into dangerous waters. The downside lies in the fact that SAP itself has difficulty filling its consulting positions with competent people. Sometimes, projects are scoped by SAP consultants whose interests are more in the "pre-sales" arena and less in the "reality" zone, leaving consultants to face clients' unreal expectations.

On the whole, Team SAP is a welcome change to the firm's way of doing business. SAP has replaced its uneasy, arms-length, distance from implementation with a cozier, more professional approach and continues to leave the lion's share of the consulting burden to its alliance partners.

Horizontal Solutions for Vertical Markets

For months on end, the SAP world has waited with baited breath for the roll-out of SAP R/3 version 4. This is the version that is 'componentized' and 'vertical'. What that first word means is that the whole enchilada of R/3 can now be broken down into digestible taquitos (financials, logistics, et al can now be upgraded independently rather than the whole hog). The vertical notion is what excites the market, as SAP will now be offering specific R/3 product to various industries like retail, public works, healthcare, oil and gas, automotive and more. A few years ago, it seemed laughable to see lists of SAP 'target' markets and find that virtually every possible market in the world was listed. However, that mountain range of R&D pfennigs is yielding tangible results and the laughter is turning, albeit slowly, to a smile.

More Wives than Brigham Young

SAP maintains active partnerships with Pandesic, Oracle, IBM, Hewlett Packard, Intellicorp, Microsoft, iXos, Sun, four of the Big 6, Digital, Compaq, and a panoply of others. These partnerships are not merely strategic, but touch upon platforms, applications, add-on functions, communications, and every other facet of the product and company. In particular SAP is tightly coiled with Microsoft, Oracle, Hewlett Packard, and IBM and, with its size, is now a permanent fixture on the scene.

The Pandesic partnership is actually a 50%-50% joint venture between Intel and SAP. Pandesic has developed an Internet commerce or electronic commerce solution for companies. This joint venture is a clear sign of SAP's awareness of the import of the Internet and the choice of Intel as a partner (rather than a host of other candidates) is intriguing.

Years ago, the term 'PC-compatible' was bandied about, and that term coalesced into Microsoft compatible. In similar fashion, great numbers of software firms are now offering SAP complements, with SAP's blessing, so the term 'SAP-compatible' has actually been heard in more than one office.

In sum, SAP will be around for the duration of your career and mine, not only continuing its rapid rate of new license sales but also continuing its breakneck pace in offering industry-specific solutions, implementation accelerators, and more connectivity.

Competitors like Baan, Oracle, and PeopleSoft may continue to make collective inroads in the market share for client/server software but, most especially on a global level, SAP will remain at the summit for years to come.

It is not just "the next hot thing" because it is ever evolving, both through SAP's new releases and through licensing firms' ability to configure and reconfigure it to fit the face of changing business conditions.

Though some analysts feel that SAP will become the Microsoft of applications software, other software solutions will continue to exist and to serve. SAP's current international reign is only about four years old and will certainly be challenged by its competitors in years to come. This is to the good. And when Bill Gates is deservedly taken in leg shackles to a squalid prison off the coast of Seattle (with a life sentence that includes watching 'Citizen Kane' twice each day) we will see a similar healthy competition for micro-software (and maybe a new operating system named Rosebud).

In the interim, do not worry yourself with what comes after SAP. It might well be more SAP.

Afterward: Nostalgia Isn't What It Used to Be

The abused notion of 'change' is at the heart of SAP, and we have all read and heard enough about the necessity of change in contemporary business. From the stress on *radical change* by Michael Hammer to the repetitions of the word *revolution* by countless others, we are constantly being exhorted to 'get with it', 'get off the track and onto the highway', to revitalize ourselves and the companies we work in.

This is not a new message. Business journals from the 1930s are filled with similar sentiments. What distinguishes this era from that and other eras is the urgency with which the message is being carried and the relative collapse of time allowed us to hear the message and act upon it.

And how do we react? How do we change? Ten years ago, we were told that Total Quality Management would lead us there; clearly, it has not. Revolutionary theories of management, empowerment, teaming, and the like have led more to the faux-zen posturing so brilliantly ridiculed in Dilbert than to solid, lasting results. Downsizing was reworded to rightsizing and then to the very clever brightsizing, but it all came down to a process of elimination and its consequent short term compensation. Further, each of these and similar efforts to change have been *reactive*. More and more, it is no longer a question of how a firm can keep pace with change but how a firm can initiate change.

Ten years ago, Control Data, Sperry Univac, and Apple were industry giants and all that remains of them is Apple's feeble heartbeat. Ten years ago, Japan was assumed unassailable in the world of semiconductors and now Intel rules the roost. Andy Grove of that firm coined the phrase "Only the paranoid survive" and it is as apt a phrase for the end of the millennium as can be found.

My father proudly worked in the same firm for more than forty years and is hard-pressed to understand that at age forty-five, I need two hands to count up past employers. "Serving You Since 1906" or "Seventy-five years of experience in ___" are no longer significant company attributes.

In business, permanence is obsolete. Change and engines for change are now business necessities. Traditional information systems cannot support change; indeed, maintaining such systems condemns a firm to an inability to change with the necessary speed. Such firms are future Sperry Univacs and Control Datas (two firms who failed to foresee the extinction of the mainframe). All companies are endangered; all workers are challenged to maintain their positions and to do so they must adapt to change in ever diminishing timescales.

SAP's R/3, with its client/server and open systems architecture, (to name only one key attribute) enables change. Actually, enable is too weak a word. What an R/3 project does: a) it forces an initial, often radical change, and then b) perpetuates the engine of change.

The nerds are still around and that is all to the good, provided that they alone are not controlling the destiny of your business software. Indeed, it is through the efforts of these nerds (who are, after all, just folks) that the breakthroughs described in this book have occurred.

However, if you have a yearning to slip the surly bonds of traditional IS systems and provide your enterprise the wherewithal to move ahead, hearken to the messages of this book. Many of these messages apply to any enterprise-wide solution, not just SAP. Workflow is your destination and you will approach it from a horizontal position.

May your business, and your satisfaction, flow...

SAP P.S.

- ⌐ Red Light, Green Light: Are You Ready?

- ⌐ Alternative Life Styles

- ⌐ SAP Competitors

- ⌐ Useful Web Sites

- ⌐ SAP Newsgroups

- ⌐ SAP Bibiliography

- ⌐ Glossary of Terms

Red Light, Green Light: Are You Ready?

Not every firm is capable of successfully carrying out an SAP endeavor. Indeed, many firms have a structure, a culture, or a management style which will sabotage any such undertaking.

Between the poles of "red light" and "green light" are several shaded hues, but let us first take a look at the poles.

Red Light

Firms built by acquisition have difficulties 'getting horizontal' if true operational mergers have not taken place after the acquisitions. This is most telling in firms that diversified in the 1980's and now have disparate, loosely-associated commercial activities. Divisional chief executives are not prone to flattening their management if that flattening includes their own selves.

Family-owned companies tend to be the farthest behind in the technology curve and thus tend to have greater chasms to cross if they are to reach the land of Ess Ay Pee. Worse, family-owned companies also tend to rely on their traditions, thus hampering business process reengineering.

In similar fashion, firms with an employee base with a high average of years of service tend to resist the changes inherent in such an undertaking. Recent hires tend to see company weaknesses as soluble; old hands have long since viewed those weaknesses as company characteristics. Admittedly, such an employee base can exist because of a high degree of faith in the company; this faith, combined with management commitment, can turn the tide.

Managers looking for a quick fix will have clearly misunderstood the nature of the SAP beast and will probably be devoured by it.

Green Light

Global firms which have struggled with knotty problems like multi-level accounting, language, consolidation nightmares, currency differences, and the like tend to leap to SAP because it addresses those problems head on.

Firms that are facing extinction can succeed because the sense of urgency lends impetus to decision-making, compromise, and the radical change that SAP can foster. Dithering, tinkering, dabbling, and putzing around are not options for firms on the brink of failure.

New firms (i.e. less than ten years old) tend to have flexible employees and fewer stultifying traditions to hold them back.

Firms with unified management whose members share a profit motive (e.g. partnerships) tend to understand the benefits of workflow and react favorably to launching a project that will enable it.

Firms with managers who are unanimously fed up with a long cycle of failed IT projects (perceived or real) tend to look favorably on SAP as an alternative to 'all that.' This type of firm slips back toward yellow light status if these managers lose patience too quickly.

Firms which have enthusiastically undertaken other major projects and succeeded at the majority of them are deep green when it comes to SAP. Even those firms which have tended to leap into trendy new business initiatives of dubious value (Total Quality Management comes to mind) will at least have a culture of experimentation and innovation; more so than timorous, conservative firms.

Changing the Lights from **Red** to **Green**

If you have found yourself in the red light section (uh, rephrase that to red light category), or somewhere in between, you might still prepare yourselves for an SAP undertaking by first making an inventory of your relative strengths and weaknesses. The areas of your enterprise to include in such an inventory are:

Company strategy: Do you have one? Is it really a strategy, or is it just a list of resolutions and good intentions?

Your Current IS: Is it a disaster or is it simply insufficient? (Note: it is easier to digest an SAP project if your current systems are awful. There's a lot less moaning amongst the ranks about losing the 'good old' systems.)

Company Structure: Is your company coherently structured with clear reporting lines and authorities? A test: how long does it take you to explain your company structure to someone from the outside? If more than ten minutes, you may have a problem (and it may be a problem that such a project will help unravel).

Employee Readiness: How eager will the employee populace be if you announce that you are going to reengineer your business processes and implement R/3 to support a new organization? By the same token, do you have sufficient employee expertise for such an evolutionary step?

Company Attitude Re Systems: Are there any Smith Corona typewriters in your office? How about a Rolodex? Adding machines, punch cards, carbon paper? If you are moving from largely manual and batch systems to R/3, a serious education bridge will have to be crossed.

Management Style: How wide is the gulf between senior management and the basic employee populace? Ivory towers are brought low by an SAP project. How cohesive are your management groups? Lack of consensus (and/or discipline) will turn an ASAP project into Project Infinity. (Psst...blame the consultants.)

Financial Posture: cutting corners on an SAP project is ill-advised.

Recent Company History: If your company has successfully completed other major projects in the past three or four years, you may be in a strong position to undertake this one. If your company is incessantly launching and dropping initiatives, think again. (As mentioned earlier, the classic cost driver for SAP projects is the start-stop-restart cycle of companies that do not know beforehand what they are getting into.)

Some firms, finding themselves unprepared for an SAP project, take four to six months to attack their weaknesses and then begin. Such preparation, usually education-based, is time well spent and the investment pays off in spades once the project has begun in vigor.

Alternative Life Styles

Your systems are old and no longer provide the support you need. Your company is in a growth mode and it is time for you to replace those legacy systems wholesale. No more tinkering, no more fiddling around. It is decision time. Get out the software brochures and surf the Net...Baan, Peoplesoft, SAP, Oracle, QAD, Abacus...dynamic data, data warehousing, dynamic data warehousing, zippo zing dynamo data, zero sum integration model, integro data dynamics. After a few hours, your eyes glaze over.

The project phase in which the most dithering occurs is usually this one in which at least three candidates are identified and then compared and contrasted to the nth degree. Unfortunately, far too much of this study still centers on functionality, but we are no longer in a phase of business in which it suffices to create a decision matrix like the one below. Functional contrasts are only a subset of the decision table.

There are countless viable alternatives to SAP. In a succeeding section, we offer a list and description of key competitors, all of which offer software and services that are top of the line. However, you must first consider the strategy that you will follow. These tend to break down into the following:

1. We Did It All Ourselves

2. Current Systems + Package Software + Interfacing

3. SAP + Packages and/or Homemade + Interfacing

4. All best-of-breed, all interfaced.

Option 1 is so wrongheaded and passe that it hardly requires commentary. Homemade systems for all applications made some sense twenty-five years ago, when package software was in its infancy. The companies that have continued down this path usually do so because of an over-developed sense of their uniqueness in the world of business (or an overbearing systems manager who cannot face the abandonment of a lifetime of design and development).

Option 2 is the reality of the vast majority of businesses. It is an option forced by circumstance and evolution. As discussed in the opening chapter, the flexibility of this strategy is undercut by the high burden of maintaining interfaces, particularly if you seek a high degree of integration.

Option 3 is the dip-your-toe-in-the-water option. It is usually followed by firms with weak or indecisive management teams who settle differences with compromises. It is a mistake to take a small piece of SAP and plug it into your family of heterogenous applications. One module alone may function wonderfully, but all benefit of enterprise-wide vision is lost: no natural integration (your interfaces would not compare favorably) and no homogeneity of utilization. The final result is something like the hybrid thing that the Alien Mom gave birth to in the film *Alien Resurrection*: vaguely human, but really ugly.

Option 4 has been chosen by few firms but seems to be a horizon that the industry is drifting toward. As worldwide standards are being established for communications and connectivity, it is believed that interfacing will be vastly simplified and that clients will be able to plug business modules from diverse suppliers into a coherent company whole without the interfacing nightmares being faced today. The rise of BAPI's (Business Application Programming Interfaces) lends to the credence of this point of view. BAPIs are *public* interfaces that are developed in conjunction with SAP customers, Microsoft, and standards organizations. Think of them as islands between diverse systems that allow for the sharing of software objects and data. Over the next five years or so, we will continue to see progress in this regard and the option of picking and choosing amongst best-of-breed software modules may be viable.

Major alternatives, in the world of client/server competitors, are Baan, PeopleSoft, and Oracle. In 1997, these three combined had only 20% of the client/server application market, whereas SAP alone had 30%.

SAP Competitors

When it comes to package software, comparison shopping is a corporate tradition. The majority of clients will cull a short list from a variety of vendors and then compare the final candidates in terms of functionality, cost, the reliability of the vendor, etc.

For those of you who are still stuck in the decision process, this section offers a list of client/server software vendors that could be considered competitors of SAP.

Main Competitors:

PEOPLE SOFT www.peoplesoft.com
A phenomenal company, PeopleSoft was launched in 1987 but did not register on the vendor map until about 1992. With projected income of around $750M for 1997, it is dwarfed by SAP on a global scale but is holding its own in North America.

Its software applications consists of manufacturing, distribution, finance, human resource and PeopleTools modules. Since HRMS was its first product, it has a strong HR reputation, but this is a North American HR, not suitable for global use.

BAAN www.baan.com
This Dutch-based company is a worldwide provider of enterprise-wide business software applications and has made rapid strides in North America since 1994. Many companies in the hybrid manufacturing, automotive, electronics and process industries use this kind of software. BAAN applications include: manufacturing, project, finance, service, process, distribution and transportation modules.

ORACLE www.oracle.com
Larry Ellison's empire reported $4.2 billion in earnings for 1996, of which 54% were tagged as 'software licenses and other'. Oracle is also involved in consulting, networking, EDMS, and databases.

Its software applications include manufacturing, finance, project systems, human resource, market management and service. It is particularly strong in the areas of manufacturing, finance and human resource.

Oracle is also a technology partner to both SAP and BaaN. It is the people's choice of databases to work with R/3. Thus, applications sales folks who lose out to SAP are often comforted by the fact that at least their database was sold.

Others

ADAGE www.sctcorp.com/adage.html
Their offering is an object-based, fully graphical Enterprise Resource Planning software designed for global manufacturing and distribution enterprises serving the process industries. ADAGE is configured to run on Microsoft SQL Server, Oracle and Ingres databases. Operating systems supported include NT, UNIX, and HP-UX. ADAGE is also capable of running on Windows NT or Windows 95 environments.

ABACUS Research AG www.abacus.ch (in German)
A Swiss firm offering multi-application software. They have a solid reputation for financials and human resources.

AVALON www.avalon.com
Supports extensive external communications capabilities which can run on a Windows 95, Windows NT or internet browser. The software includes modules for manufacturing, planning, finance, and Avalon architecture.

CINCOM www.cincom.com
Financial and manufacturing-based mission-critical software for application development, document management, database management and enterprise business application systems.

DATALOGIX INTERNATIONAL
www.hp.com/solcat/company/46759.html
This firms offers process-manufacturing software that fully integrates manufacturing, quality management, customer service, financial and regulatory solutions.

DUN & BRADSTREET www.dbsoftware.com
Long-regarded as the king of financials, this group has expanded its offering to include human resource, management and finance, decision support, budgets and procurements.

MARCAM www.marcam.com
This firm offers an object-oriented application set for manufacturing, logistics, maintenance and finance. It also has modules that include process definition, inventory management and control modules.

QAD www.qad.com
This firm, of debatable pronunciation (kwad? cad? nope, its kew ay dee) offers software that provides organizations with an integrated global supply chain management solution that includes manufacturing, distribution, finance, service and support management applications.

Useful Web Sites

This list was compiled in the winter of 1997-98. The world wide web being what it is, there is no assurance that access to these sites will be eternal.

http://www.sap.com
This site contains a wealth of information about the company, the product, services, platforms, you name it. There are continual announcements that have the feel of SAP chest-thumping, but the sheer depth and span of this site is impressive.

http://www.sapsource.com
The author's firm's website, including white papers, links, a monthly newsletter, recruitment postings, and information about publications, seminars, and general SAP education.

http:// www. sap-faq.html (SAP FAQ'S)
The most complete site there is, including masses of data regarding the product, the company, technical and functional details, books, training, and more.

http:// www.softwarejobs.com
This is the site for Allen Davis & Associates, which is a recruiting firm. In the SAP section of this site, managed by the talented Jon Reed is an absolute wealth of information about SAP consulting, placement, work visas, rates and negotiations, the consulting market, and interviews with SAP insiders.

http:/www.ie.iwi.unibe.ch/sap/
This site is for the curious shopper, as it contains news, white papers, gifs, all sorts of odds and ends, though a majority of the information is in German.

SAP News Groups

The following newsgroups can be found on Usenet:

de.alt.comp.sap-r3 This group is used for information sharing and the posting of queries or SOS calls about the software, Recruiting agencies sometimes jump in and for some reason there are a number of postings for 'adult' groups.

Sample posting:

> Projects in Seoul, South Korea!
> Senior consultants with following skills are required:
> 1. Solid R3 SD   (for 6 months)
> 2. Experienced project manager (6-7 months)
> 3. SIS for 1-2 months
> Good rates + expenses.

comp.soft-sys.bus.sap This group tends to be job posting for consultants and headhunters intermingled with information sharing.

Sample posting:

> I am having a problem, the first logon screen i get is in german, and only when i login as SAP*, i get my menu in englsh. can somebody pl tell me how to get the first logon screen in english?

This newsgroup is offered by Realtime USA which has a web site at www.realtimeusa.com that offers a directory search of SAP consultancies (which beats using a search engine) and an SAP web site spider.

SAP Bibliography

Until the arrival of the first edition of Nancy Bancroft's book (listed here) in the fall of 1996, the only source of printed information about SAP, in English, was the supplier itself. While Ms. Bancroft's book remains the standard,, more and more books have followed and even more are listed at Amazon Books as due for arrival. The majority of the books are technical manuals such as ABAP/4 guides. The following is a select list of worthwhile books for business people whose interests are not technical. All of them can be easily ordered through Amazon Books (amazon.com) or Cary Prague (caryp.com).

Implementing SAP R/3 : How to Introduce a Large System into a Large Organization, 2nd Edition
by Nancy H. Bancroft, Henning Seip, Andrea Sprengel
2nd Edition Hardcover, 336 pages
Published by Prentice Hall (September 1997)
Dimensions (in inches): 9.30 x 7.27 x .99
ISBN: 013889213X
Subject: Architecture, business context, applications, and implementation of R/3; the standard textbook, a must.

In the Path of the Whirlwind: An Apprentice Guide to the World of SAP by Michael Doane
3rd Edition, Mass Market Paperback, 140 pages
Published by The Consulting Alliance (March 1997)
ISBN: 1575790297
Subject: what is R/3, the costs, how to implement, etc. for beginners

Capturing the Whirlwind: Your Field Guide to a Successful SAP Implementation by Michael Doane
2nd Edition, Mass Market Paperback, 166 pages
Published by The Consulting Alliance (April 1997)
ISBN: 1575790300
Subject: Management and team field guide for planning through post-implementation

SAP R/3 System : A Client/Server Technology
by Rudiger Buck-Emden, Jurgen Galimow, Sap AgList: $29.95
Hardcover, 255 pages
Published by Addison-Wesley Pub Co (August 1, 1996)
Dimensions (in inches): 9.56 x 6.94 x .69
ISBN: 0201403501
Subject: Client/server technology, architecture, and applications

10 Minute Guide to SAP R/3
by Simon Sharpe, Deanna
Paperback, 208 pages
Published by Que Education & Training (March 1997)
Dimensions (in inches): 8.43 x 5.55 x .52
ISBN: 0789708981
Subject: Navigation and applications for end users

SAP Documentation and Training Development Guide
by Kathryn E. Park, Robert S. Park 1 Edition
Paperback, 192 pages
Published by BobKat Press (May 1, 1997)
ISBN: 0965662128
Subject: Documentation standards and training guide

Special Edition Using SAP R/3 : The Most Complete Reference
by Asap World Consultancy 2nd Bk&cdr Edition
Hardcover, 1202 pages
Published by Que Education & Training (August 1, 1997)
Dimensions (in inches): 9.47 x 7.77 x 2.22
ISBN: 0789713519
Subject: as stated, a huge SAP reference, but also includes great
detail about the consulting world

Other related books

The SAP Consultant Handbook: Your Sourcebook to Lasting Success in an SAP Career
by Jon Reed and Michael Doane
1st Edition, Mass Market Paperback,
Published by DA Press (Oct. 1998)
ISBN: not yet issued
Subject: breaking into SAP consulting and succeeding in it

Best Practices in Reengineering : What Works and What Doesn't in the Reengineering Process
by David K. Carr, Henry J. Johansson
Hardcover, 235 pages
Published by McGraw-Hill
Publication date: April 1, 1995
Dimensions (in inches): 9.27 x 6.24 x .94
ISBN: 007011224X

Glossary of Terms

ABAP/4	Advanced Business Application Programming Language (4th level)
AM	Fixed Assets Management application in SAP
ASAP	the Accelerated SAP method
AS-IS	a study of current ways of working, culminating in charts and scripts to be thrown away. Usually precedes a TO BE phase
Basis	The middleware that manages client/server functions across R/3
Business Process	a group or series of activities by which inputs are turned to outputs that benefit the customer
C/S	Client/server
CBS	Certified Business Solutions (SAP program for small firms)
CO	Controlling application in SAP R/3
Configure	filling in R/3 tables (and appropriate combinations) to make the software work as desired
Customize	Effect changes to SAP software so it will fit your process designs
FI	Financial application in SAP R/3
Gap analysis	What you want less what R/3 can do for you = gap analysis (usually off the mark)
GUI	Graphical User Interface
HR	Human Resources application in SAP R/3
ICOE	Industry Centers of Expertise (e.g. Oil & Gas, Automotive, Health Care)
Interfaces	Program-driven connections between disparate data bases
IS	Information systems
IS	Industry Solutions application in SAP
IT	Information technology
Middleware (Basis)	The / between client and server, as in Client/Server

MM	Materials management application in R/3
PM	Production Maintenance application in SAP R/3
Portability	the capacity of software to run on operating systems from disparate platform suppliers
PP	Production Planning application in SAP R/3
PS	Project System application in SAP R/3
QA	Quality Assurance in SAP R/3
QM	Quality Management application in SAP R/3
SAP	Pronounced Ess Ay Pee; the supplier
SD	Sales and distribution application in SAP R/3
Software suite	Multiple software applications derived from common design
TO BE	the charting and scripting of new business processes

A Note About the Typeface

Some of the most popular typefaces in history are those based on the types of the sixteenth-century printer, publisher, and type designer Claude Garamond. His oldstyle designs, based on the Aldine model used by Venetian printers from the end of the previous century, dominated the composing rooms of printers well into the 18th century.

Characteristic of Garamond's original typefaces is High Renaissance forms with moderate contrast and long extenders, but the smaller eye of its letters gives it a graceful look that helps it stand out from the pack of modern Garamonds.

Ordering Information

Direct order: send a fax to (605) 367-1169 or an e-mail to micdoane@aol.com

Provide:

Quantity	Unit Cost
1-5	$24.95
6-20	$21.95
21+	$20.95

Plus shipping

⌐ Your Name
⌐ Business Name (optional)
⌐ Delivery Address
⌐ Invoice Address (if other than delivery address)
⌐ Delivery Method   (Standard mail, Fedex, other)
⌐ Quantity Ordered
⌐ Phone (for assured delivery)

You will be billed when books are delivered.

Order Online:

E-mail to caryp@caryp.com
or call 800 277-3117 or order online at www.caryp.com

ISBN: 1-57579-125-0

This book is not available in bookstores

About the Author:

Michael Doane is a senior manager with Grant Thornton LLP. He has twenty-five years of business systems experience in the U.S., Europe, and Asia.

He is the author of *In the Path of the Whirlwind, An Apprentice Guide to the World of SAP* and *Capturing the Whirlwind, Your Field Guide to a Successful SAP Implementation*. He can be reached via e-mail at micdoane@aol.com.

Contributors:

Betty Costa is a senior manager at Grant Thornton LLP. Eight of her twenty years of experience have been dedicated to the management of SAP implementation projects.

Nancy Bancroft is the author of the celebrated *Implementing SAP R/3, How to Introduce a Large System into a Large Organization*. She can be reached at bancroft@rmi.com.

Mark Dendinger is the president of Holland Technology Group, which is a national implementation partner with SAP. Holland was awarded the first Certified Business Solutions Provider of the Year Award for 1997 by SAP AG.

Jon Reed is an SAP consulting recruiter at Allen Davis & Associates. His website at softwarejobs.com is a gold mine of information about SAP consulting.

David Chapman is the IS Manager and SAP Project Manager for Lyondell-Citgo Refining Company Limited.

Peter Steiner is the SAP Project Manager for Hercules, Incorporated, which is completing a global roll-out of SAP R/3.

Carol Martin is the SAP Training Leader for Hercules, Incorporated.